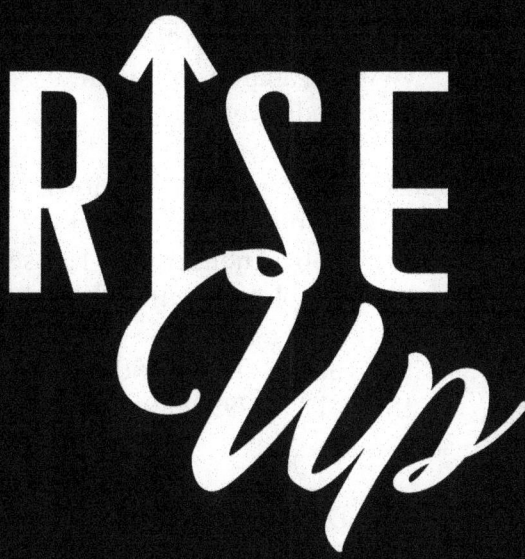

Copyright Notice

Rise Up
by Cassandra Woods

© 2018 Cassandra Woods
www.cassandrawoods.com
info@cassandrawoods.com

Published by Anointed Fire House
www.anointedfirehouse.com
Cover Design by Anointed Fire House
Author photograph by Heather Whidden

ISBN-13: 978-0-9993380-6-3
ISBN-10: 0-9993380-6-4

DISCLAIMER

This book contains material protected under International and Federal Copyright Laws and Treaties. Any unauthorized reprint or use of this material is prohibited. No part of this book may be reproduced or transmitted in any form or by any means, electronic or mechanical, including photocopying, recording, or by any information storage and retrieval system without express written permission from the author/publisher.

I have tried to recreate events, locales and conversations from my memories of them. In order to maintain their anonymity in some instances, I have changed the names of individuals and places and I may have changed some identifying characteristics and details such as physical properties, occupations and places of residence.

Although the author and publisher have made every effort to ensure that the information in this book was correct at press time, the author and publisher do not assume and hereby disclaim any liability to any party for any loss, damage, or disruption caused by errors or omissions, whether such errors or omissions result from negligence, accident, or any other cause.

Scripture quotations, marked NIV are taken from The Holy Bible, New International Version ®, NIV ®, Copyright 1973, 1978, 1984, 2001 by Biblica, Inc.™ Used by permission. All rights reserved.

Scripture quotations, marked NLT are taken from The Holy Bible, New Living Translation, Copyright© 1996. Used by permission of Tyndale House Publishers, Inc., Wheaton, Illinois 60189. All rights reserved.

Scripture quotations marked ESV are taken from The Holy Bible, English Standard Version®. English Standard Version are registered trademarks of Crossway®.

Holy Bible: The Message (the Bible in contemporary language). 2005. Colorado Springs, CO: NavPress. As found in BibleGateway.com.

DEDICATION

I dedicate this book to my husband, Christopher, who has always believed in me and supported my dream to write. Additionally, I dedicate this book to my daughter, Courtney, for her unwavering encouragement, my sons - Clinton, for his motivating talks, Clifton, for his Spirit-inspired words, and Caleb, for his generous hugs. I also dedicate this book to my parents, Willie and Geraldine, who made me believe that I could accomplish whatever I wanted to do. To all of you, your encouragement, prayers, support and sacrifice have been instrumental in this book coming to light. Thank you.

Acknowledgments

Thank you to Cindy Willingham and my writing sisters at Breath on Paper Blog, who provided me an opportunity to rekindle the fire of writing inside of me. Thank you to Tiffany Buckner for her editing and inspiration. Thank you to Cheryl Lundy for her insight and encouragement. Thank you to God who sustains me and everyone who said a prayer for me and my writing. A special thank you to ProFreshional Creations.

Table of Contents

Introduction XIII

Chapter 1
Rise Up and Know God 1

Chapter 2
Rise Up and Believe 23

Chapter 3
Rise Up and Pray 39

Chapter 4
Rise Up to Freedom 55

Chapter 5
Rise Up in Peace 71

Chapter 6
Rise Up on Purpose 87

Chapter 7
Rise Up to Identity 103

Chapter 8
Rise Up to Covenant 117

Chapter 9
Rise Up and Rest 133

Chapter 10
Rise Up to Success 149

Final Message CLXVII

Introduction

Have you experienced some difficult times? Are you in the midst of a problem and don't know how it will be resolved? Do your challenges seem to continue with no end in sight? Have you wondered when things were going to change for the better? If so, this book is for you. Many of us have been taught that we have to wait on God. We've heard that God is sovereign and everything will happen according to his will. Though there is some truth to these statements, they are not complete. This type of thinking leads to a lot of unaccomplished goals, misdirected lives and early departures from Earth. The missing truth in this statement is that God can do everything if he wants to, but he purposely designed us and gave us everything we need to cooperate with him to bring his will to light in the world. We are co-laborers with Christ. There are some things that won't happen if we don't do our parts. Rise up and join me in looking at ten keys of truth that will allow us to work together with God by contributing our best, in an effort to achieve God's plan.

Chapter 1

Rise Up and Know God

"Be still, and know that I am God..."
– Psalm 46:10

After a recent hospital stay, I decided enough is enough. I am a Christian. I am going to church, serving the Lord and loving his people. I am reading the Bible, listening for God's voice and walking in his ways. Yet and still, I had another physical challenge to show up in my body that led to a ten-day hospital stay. It's just not right. There are some things the Bible talks about and God promises that I do not always see in my life or the lives of many of the people who confess to be Christians.

The Bible says:
> "Praise the Lord. Blessed are those who fear the Lord, who find great delight in his commands...Wealth and riches are in their houses, and their righteousness endures forever."
> *– Psalm 112:1-3 (NIV)*

> *"Worship the LORD your God, and his blessing will be on your food and water. I will take away sickness from among you."*
> *– Exodus 23:25 (NIV)*

> *"Take delight in the Lord, and he will give you the desires of your heart."*
> *– Psalm 37:4 (NIV)*

If you aren't familiar with these scriptures, know that they really are in the book, the Bible, which is the manual to introduce us to Jesus Christ and instruct us on how to live the life he has designed for us. Up until this point, it honestly seems as if some of us have been:

> *"Having a form of godliness but denying its power. Have nothing to do with such people."*
> *– 2 Timothy 3:5-6 (NIV)*

This scripture sounds serious. The Bible is telling us to have nothing to do with this kind of people. I found myself asking: *Am I the person people should have nothing to do with?* Are you? Disturbing perhaps, but the truth is we must ask ourselves some hard questions. Are we truly experiencing the things the Bible speaks about or are we just talking about them?

My husband and I walked through a long financial trial. We had started a business, worked hard, had some significant success and then, after more than 20 years, we watched our contracts be canceled, business dry up and associates scatter. We had to let go of our employees and sell our company's office. Though disappointments and thoughts of failure loomed, we committed to pray and seek God's direction. God provided for our needs and a few years later, he brought us financial relief.

Also, after taking a medical test nearly twenty years ago, I spoke to a doctor and heard a word no one wants to hear about themselves. Malignant. I was in shock in that surreal moment. Although God has sustained and blessed me to continue serving him with peace and joy, my doctor has yet to give me the words I want to hear, which are: all clear. I know that the Word of God says that I have been healed by Jesus' stripes and I receive my healing by faith. However, I have been walking it out for a long time.

The Bible calls it working out my salvation. I am not complaining though. I am thankful to be here, thankful for my healing and thankful for all God has taught me during these years.

I understand that we will face trials, but I've learned that how we walk them out is very important. Are we walking as an overcomer or a victim? We have a choice. It's so easy to become accustomed to suffering when going through a trial, especially when it lasts a long time. But if we choose to be overcomers, we can't stay down. When the trial is over and sometimes, even as it continues, we have to rise up. Join me.

To start the journey of truth, we must first know who we're dealing with. I have often heard people who are discussing potential business or personal relationships say something similar. First, they give a long or short explanation of their experiences with a person, followed by "I just want you to know who you're dealing with." Who is God? Is he just someone we talk about at church? Does he really want to be involved in my life?

The Bible tells us so much about God, the I Am that I Am. I think we should start there. I believe we can learn a lot about God by studying his names. He has several. After all, what's in a name? Typically, everyone is given a name at birth. However, I do recall Author and International Speaker, Christine Caine, saying that on the official paperwork that was completed after her birth, she was listed as Unnamed until she was adopted.[1] Fortunately, as a baby, she didn't know, but imagine what Unnamed represents. Perhaps she did not receive the motherly bonding that many of us did. Perhaps she could sense the lack of love. I don't really know, but I do know that we all tend to like our names. Remember that "a person's name is to that person the sweetest and most important sound in any language."[2]

Let's take a look at some of the names of God.

Adonai

This name means Lord and Master. Let's examine the meaning of Lord in general. According to Dictionary.com, a lord is "a person who has authority, control, or power over others; a master, chief, or ruler." This means that God expects to have authority and power over those of us who call him Lord.

> *"Why do you call me, 'Lord, Lord,' and do not do what I say?"*
> *– Luke 6:46 (NIV)*

Our lives should be less of us and more of him. He is not really our Lord if we don't obey him.

Now let's move on to Master. Google's dictionary lists the definition of master as "a man who has people working for him, especially servants or slaves."

> *"The wife of a man from the company of the prophets cried out to Elisha, "Your servant my husband is dead, and you know that he revered the LORD. But now his creditor is coming to take my two boys as his slaves."*
> *– 2 Kings 4:1 (NIV)*

This woman was concerned about her boys being enslaved as a payment for her dead husband's debt.

It was customary in the biblical days for people to pay off debt by selling themselves into slavery to the person they were indebted to. However, every seven years, in the year of Jubilee, all debt was to be canceled (Deuteronomy15:1, Leviticus 25:39-40).

We are indebted to God for all he has done for us. It's not enough to just invite Jesus into our hearts, unless you just want a ticket into heaven. Some people want him to participate in all of their plans and have no intention of doing life his way. But if we want a ticket and the experience of living a victorious life on Earth, it's going to cost us more. We must become bondslaves of Christ. We're going to have to be willing to put his will for us before our own, just as Jesus did in the Garden of Gethsemane when he prayed,

> *"Father, if you are willing, take this cup from me; yet not my will, but yours be done."*
> *– Luke 22:42 (NIV)*

He said this as the pain and humiliation of death on the cross awaited him. At times, there will be things that God directs us to do or not to do that will conflict with our own desires. If Jesus is our Lord, we will choose to follow his direction. The choice of going our own way in opposition to his leading is called sin. Scripture tells us that:

> *"Sin shall no longer be your master, because you are not under the law, but under grace."*
> *– Romans 6:14 (NIV)*

Who is your master?

El Shaddai

This name means God Almighty. It indicates that God is omnipotent, all-powerful. Wouldn't you want to serve someone like that? Think of those childhood fights. I know they are a lot different today than when most of us were growing up. If you happen to watch the news, you may conclude that innocent spats between two kids have turned into gun-toting teenagers willing to take the lives of one another for minuscule reasons. In my elementary years, the people who knew they had a big brother or sister who would come to their aid were more likely to challenge someone to a fight.

Think about it. When we obey God's commands, we have an all-powerful God who is willing to stand for us. We don't have to fear anything because whatever we need, he's got it. It reminds me of a stanza of a song written by Bill and Gloria Gaither that says, "Because He lives, I can face tomorrow. Because He lives, all fear is gone."

On a cruise ship, people are enjoying the pool, planned events, meals, theater and just relaxing on deck, among other things, while the Captain guides the ship. They are not worried. They have relinquished control to the Captain. They trust that he has the best interest of the passengers in mind and that he will guide them in the way they should go. They believe he will successfully maneuver the ship through threats of pirates and storms. God wants to do this for us every day of our lives.

Who is guiding your life?

Jehovah Nissi

Have you ever watched a parade and seen the band or organization approaching with someone carrying a banner identifying the organization? The banner displays to the crowd who is coming. I believe when we decide to walk in faith and believe for everything Jesus paid the price for us to live in, we should have a banner.

What banner should go before us, announcing our arrival or identity? There are banners for sports teams, little leagues and all the way up to professionals. Companies use them to help market their businesses.

"According to the Book of Exodus in the Bible, Jehovah-Nissi is the name given by Moses to the altar which he built to celebrate the defeat of the Amalekites at Rephidim."[3] How awesome is that? Take your banner and fly it for all the victories you have won with God.

I have previously done a couple of walks as a breast cancer survivor. However, that's not my identity. I am more than a survivor. I am a thriver. I am an overcomer. I am a warrior. I am more than a conqueror. I felt God was telling me to see myself as He sees me. I am healed, restored, strengthened, established and confirmed by God.

What battles have you overcome? What battles are you currently in that, with God's help, you will win? Try these things to keep yourself focused.

1. Put a picture up of yourself looking and feeling your best. Look at it often.

2. Write down all the good things God says about you in his word. That's who you are.

What banner goes before you?

Jehovah Shammah

Think of a time when you felt at your wit's end. Your situation seemed to be more than you could bear. A sick child. A job loss. More bills than finances to pay. No escape. Life seemed to be crashing in on you. Maybe you cried out, "God, where are you?"

If you stayed connected to him, you soon realized that he was right there with you all the time. Trouble comes when we turn our focus to our problem, instead of our God.

"But seek first his kingdom and his righteous-

> ness, and all these things will be given to you as well."
> — *Matthew 6:33 (NIV)*

Now, this is a comforting scripture to know that all the things you've been worrying about will be given to you, but please don't overlook the first part of the verse. We must seek God's kingdom first, in addition to his righteousness. That is your job now. Instead of worrying, trust God and do what the scriptures tell you.

> *"Never will I leave you; never will I forsake you."*
> — *Hebrews 13:5 (NIV)*

Know that He is with you always. Wherever you go, he is there. Look for God in your situations of life. His word says to seek him with all your heart and he will be found by you.

Are you looking for God? He's right there.

Jehovah-Tsidkenu

God, our Righteousness. The righteous are those

who have been reconciled to God through Jesus Christ. They have successfully dealt with the sin that had come between themselves and God. This is one of those situations you can't fake. Well, you could but the results would be seen soon enough. I am one of those people who tries to just be me. There are times when I spiff it up for a special event or occasion, but for the most part, what you see is what you get. I believe being real is what God wants for us. He wants righteousness to rise from our core without pretense.

> *"This is the covenant I will make with them after that time, says the Lord. I will put my laws in their hearts, and I will write them on their minds."*
> – Hebrews 10:16 (NIV)

The evidence of our righteousness should come up from the center of our being; it should come from our hearts. God wants righteousness to be so much a part of us that we can't distinguish between it and us. Righteousness should be so ingrained in us that it is noticeable in our speech and our behavior.

You may be thinking that this is a lot of pressure. The truth is, we aren't living in a time that dictates that we have to run out and get an animal sacrifice to take to the priest if we fail. Since the New Testament came into effect, when you accept Jesus as your Savior and Lord, you are forever covered by the sacrifice of Jesus.

> *"For by one sacrifice he has made perfect forever those who are being made holy... This is the covenant I will make with them after that time, says the Lord. I will put my laws in their hearts, and I will write them on their minds."*
> *– Hebrews 10:14,16*

When God is the moral compass of your heart, your life of righteousness will spring forth from him. Remember that in a perfect world, your good works and doing right should come from the heart and not just outward desires, because they don't last.

Jehovah-Rapha

Our God is the God who heals. That's right. Whether you believe healing is for today or not really doesn't matter, because it's happening. In fact, I know someone who had tests done and was scheduled for surgery. When she went in for surgery they did not have to do what they expected to do, because the matter had been resolved. She had received a miraculous healing.

I, on the other hand, have dealt with a diagnosis for years. So, I did a little talking to God and a lot of research on healing and came to the conclusion that there are at least two ways God heals. One way is immediately. That would be my first choice. The second way is by process as I call it. Do you remember the ten lepers who called out to Jesus for mercy? Jesus simply responded, "Go show yourself to the priests." As they went, they were cleansed. They obeyed and were healed.

Whatever you do, don't get it twisted. God is not trying to teach you something by making you sick. That's not to say that we can't learn something going through the process. But this is not why sickness comes.

Sickness is always from the devil. If you don't

believe this, you won't be able to pray the prayer of faith. "If it be thy will," is not as effective as praying in agreement with God's word. You must know God's will to pray in faith.

> *"He himself bore our sins" in his body on the cross, so that we might die to sins and live for righteousness; "by his wounds you have been healed."*
>
> *– I Peter 2:24 (NIV)*

Saying that God may not want you to be healed is in direct contradiction to his word. Why would he send Jesus to take the stripes on his back to heal us if he didn't want us to be healed? The price has been paid. If I offer you a gift and you don't make any effort to receive it, you won't get the benefit of it. In the same way, we must learn to receive what belongs to us. Leave nothing on the table. God wants us to be well. In fact, Jesus shed his blood on the cross to pay for your sins and your sickness. It's already done.

Jehovah-Shalom

Now this right here is something to shout about.

The Lord is our peace. There is nothing we should be worried about.

> *"Therefore, I tell you, do not worry about your life..."*
> — *Matthew 6:25 (NIV)*

When God says do not do something, this implies that to do it is sin. Now, how many of us have been guilty of this before? I could raise my hand. However, as I have grown in the Lord over the years, I have learned to trust him. I know that I can depend on him to do what he said he would do. I don't have to worry.

Once, during a long hospital stay, I can remember my body was weak, but my spirit was strong. I could barely stay conscious, but when I spoke to people, I heard many encouraging words coming from my mouth. I was thinking, *who is that?* My own mind seemed surprised at the positive words I was speaking. But I knew it was the spirit inside of me. I believe the word of God that I had stored in my heart caused the Holy Spirit to rise up in me. When I was weak, He was strong.

When you regularly submit yourself to reading God's word, praying and worshiping, you are building up your spirit to rule over your mind.

> *"Do not be anxious about anything, but in every situation, by prayer and petition, with thanksgiving, present your requests to God. And the peace of God, which transcends all understanding, will guard your hearts and your minds in Christ Jesus."*
> – *Philippians 4:6-7 (NIV)*

El Qanna

"For the Lord your God is a consuming fire, a jealous God."
– *Deuteronomy 4:24 (NIV)*

A consuming fire reminds me of the California fires in October of 2017 that raged through Napa, Sonoma and more. According to Wikipedia, out of the 250 fires that started, at least two became major fires that consumed more than 245,000 acres, cost more than 3.3 billion dollars and took 44 lives.[4]

That's major.

God has a kind of righteous anger and jealousy when it comes to his children. When we decide to trust ourselves or others instead of looking to him, he is not pleased. He wants us to trust his faithfulness and believe that his word is true.

Ephesians 5:22-33 uses the marriage of a man and woman to symbolize Christ being married to the church. I don't have to tell you how jealousy in marriage can cause a lot of drama. This may be the reason there are so many divorces, as well as murder-suicide killings. However, this marriage to the body of Christ is a very important covenant intended to last till death.

> *"Bring my sons from afar and my daughters from the ends of the earth—everyone who is called by my name, whom I created for my glory, whom I formed and made."*
> *– Isaiah 43:7 (NIV)*

God created us for his glory. He wants to show us off like my mom showed off her crystal collection in her curio cabinet. God also wants us to love him with all of our heart, mind, soul and strength. Anytime we give more of our hearts to any person or anything than we give to God, we provoke his jealousy. He wants to have first place in our lives.

Jehovah-Jireh

Jehovah-Jireh means God will provide. God is the source of everything we need. As the song says, whatever you need, God's got it.

Remember the feeding of the five thousand? A great multitude was following Jesus.

> "When Jesus looked up and saw a great crowd coming toward him, he said to Philip, where shall we buy bread for these people to eat?" He asked this only to test him, for he already had in mind what he was going to do."
> – John 6:5-6 (NIV)

I just love God. He always has a plan. I can see him questioning us in the circumstances that we face. Think about that the next time you have a situation arise in your life. When you feel like you don't know what to do, remember that God has a plan. Sit down and spend time in worship and prayer. Then listen for God's direction.

Imagine being Abraham, about to sacrifice your only son. When the Lord saw he was willing to obey him on that level, he really wanted to bless Abraham.

Google Dictionary states that provide means to "make available for use." It means to supply, furnish, impart or bear. How wonderful to know that God has an unlimited supply of whatever you need. Whether you need peace or a paycheck, God will provide. Do you believe?

CHAPTER 2

Rise Up and Believe

Once my family visited the Six Flags over Georgia amusement park. It was in the middle of summer and uncomfortably hot. The lines were long for many rides and the sweltering heat made it almost unbearable for me. After buying a few three-dollar cups of lemonade, I was about ready to go. That's when I remembered that we're doing it for the kids, so I hung in there.

Then someone told us about the Flash Pass. Apparently, if you pay extra, there are certain rides that you can get a specific time reservation to ride. That allows you to continue walking around and enjoying the park while waiting. When notified that your time to ride is coming up, you simply make your way to the ride and bypass the long line by entering through an adjacent pathway.

Needless to say, we purchased a Flash Pass and began to enjoy the benefits. For us to have that experience, three things had to happen. One, we had to know that the Flash Passes existed. Secondly, we had to be willing to pay the price to get one. Lastly, we had to obey; that is to follow the instructions. We had to schedule and return to the ride at the appropriate time. Doing those things allowed us to enjoy the park a lot more.

This is quite similar to being a believer of Jesus Christ.
1. Somehow, you hear about Jesus Christ. That's the good news; it's the gospel of Jesus Christ.
2. You decide to sacrifice the life you planned for the destiny God has planned for you.
3. You learn how to walk in obedience by faith.

Believer's Believe
"And we also thank God continually because, when you received the word of God, which you heard from us, you accepted it not as a human word, but as it actually is, the word of God, which is indeed at work in you who believe."
– I Thessalonians 2:13 (NIV)

Someone can expound on the truth and give their opinion on what it means. Their statements may or may not spark an aha moment in your mind. But when scripture is given, you must know enough or be willing to search the word of God to know whether the person you are listening to is speaking truth from the Bible or their own formulation of truth.

There have been a few times that I have actually tuned out on a television minister, because I didn't believe that what he was preaching was in agreement with God's word. It's so important to get the foundation right before you build.

Think of the Leaning Tower of Pisa in Italy. It still stands today, and it also still leans. Construction work began on the tower on August 14, 1173. The tilt "caused by an inadequate foundation on ground too soft on one side to properly support the structure's weight," soon became noticeable.[4] As they proceeded to build upward, the building began to sink on one side. You want to build your life on a firm foundation, on the rock, so it doesn't wash away.

It saves a lot of time and frustration to do it the right way in the beginning. But if you already have a few years and some wrong choices behind you, it's okay. Sometimes, we go through a few unplanned turns in our journeys, but God is the ultimate fixer. With Him, all things are possible. Get in relationship with his son, Jesus Christ, and you can be on your way to living the life of an overcomer.

> *"God's solid foundation stands firm, sealed with this inscription: "The Lord knows those who are his," and, "Everyone who confesses the name of the Lord must turn away from wickedness."*
> *– 2 Timothy 2:19 (NIV)*

The Lord knows who you are, and he wants you to believe he has your best interest in mind. It comes down to trusting him. You must trust somebody, whether you travel on a bus or an airplane. Many of us know very little about how an airplane stays in the sky or what to do if we had to make an emergency landing, but we will still board planes. This is trust. We are literally giving over control to whoever is charged with piloting the airplane. We choose to believe that they desire to take us on a successful journey to our destinations.

In life, we will face challenges, unfortunate circumstances, and unfair situations. Why not believe in God? That's what believer's do.

<u>Unlock God's Promises</u>
I was trying to get on a conference call. I had started a few minutes early, but I wasn't having success. *What was wrong?* I went back to check the documentation I was sent. I dialed the telephone number. It asked for an access code. I double-checked the information I'd received and pushed the numbers on the phone. No success. Fortunately, I had time to contact the host of the call and they informed me that they had sent out an incorrect access code. No matter how well I dialed those numbers on the phone, I would not have gotten access to the conference call, because I did not have the right code.

An access code, in this digital age, is much like a key to your house. Without the right key, no one can legally enter your home. Let's say that you need someone to stop by your house and pick up something for you. Without the key, there is no access.

The same is true in the kingdom of God. Our Father God has made a lot of promises, but some of them are for us when we grow up. Through maturation or revelation, we gain the key that allows us to access the blessings of God.

> *"For I know the plans I have for you," declares the LORD, "plans to prosper you and not to harm you, plans to give you hope and a future."*
> *— Jeremiah 29:11 (NIV)*

Do you believe God has a plan for **your** life? That's a good place to start. Here's the access code: FAITH.

Acting out Faith

Unlike some people, I like math. If you think about it, most times, there is always an exact answer. I like that. I suppose in some levels of math, you could run into answers of infinity, but for the basic equation, it's safe to say that what's on the left side of the equation will equal what is on the right side of the equation. It's not like philosophy, which is more subjective. It just makes sense.

Some years ago, I came across an equation for faith. Here it is.

$$\text{Faith} = \text{Belief} + \text{Corresponding Action}$$

I really like this equation. I know most equations deal with numbers, but this is one I don't think we should put aside.

Oftentimes, we think of faith as believing God. However, the Bible says that even the demons believe. So, there is obviously something more to faith for those who are children of God.

So, just what is faith? Hebrews 11:1 says, *"Now faith is the substance of things hoped for, the evidence of things not seen."*

I see a substance as something you can touch and rub on yourself or something else. For instance, lotion is a substance. Wax for your car is a substance. It is something that is tangible.

When you are hoping and believing for something based on the word of God, you begin to take action based on your hope. I remember reading about some young ladies who would prepare a "hope chest" in preparation for their future marriages. According to Wikipedia, the contents of a "hope chest" or "glory box" included typical dowry, items such as clothing (especially a special dress), table linens, towels, bed linens, quilts and occasionally dishware.

These women had faith that they would get married and they made plans. Their plans became the substance of their faith. It was something tangible, something you could see. Though they hadn't gotten married yet and you couldn't see their husbands or hold their official marriage certificates, the evidence of their faith was their belief and their actions.

If you are awaiting your knight in shining armor who will come and sweep you off your feet for a lifetime of joy and happiness, your job is to have faith. You may or may not prepare a hope chest, but you could study how to be a godly wife in preparation for that day. You could be praying that your future husband will have a desire to follow God. You could also pray that his finances are in order and that he has a good credit score. There are so many things you can do that would represent that substance of faith.

Remember, believing is great, but faith requires you to make a corresponding action. If you see the chair, you believe it will hold you up. It doesn't become faith until you take the corresponding action of sitting in the chair, thereby expressing your trust.

The Bible is just a Book
In 2013, Barna reported that "those American adults who are antagonistic to the Bible, meaning they believe the Bible to just be a book of stories and teachings written by men, and they rarely or never read the Bible" increased from 10% in 2011 to 17%.[5] To those who don't believe in Jesus Christ, the Bible is just a book. To those of us who do believe in Jesus Christ, the Bible is our life source; it

is the word of God. It is the heart of Jesus.

> *"All Scripture is inspired by God and is useful to teach us what is true and to make us realize what is wrong in our lives. It corrects us when we are wrong and teaches us to do what is right."*
> – 2 Timothy 3:16 (NLT)

If you are having a hard time with some of the things you've read here, spend some time with God and ask him about it. Honestly, it is most expedient to have an intimate relationship, spiritually speaking, with Jesus.

In order to rise up to faith, we have to believe that God's word is infallible. His word will live forever, even after heaven and earth pass away. To rise, you must trust in his word more than your own and the thoughts and beliefs of other people. Now, this isn't a problem until you come up against something that you have strong beliefs about.

People have strong beliefs about certain subjects. That's when you usually hear "God knows my heart" or "Surely, God doesn't expect me to wait until I get married."

The truth is, our desire to walk in joy and peace is compromised when we don't follow God's way. There is no way around it; we must cooperate with God in order to maximize our experience and receive his benefits.

The next time you read a scripture that brings a question to your mind, I want you to stop and talk to God about it. Tell him that you are having a difficult time with the scripture and ask him to help you process, believe and integrate it into your life.

What you don't want to do is just dismiss the scripture. It could be a valuable truth to help you move toward your destiny, or it could be a needed correction to keep your progress from being hindered.

> *"But when you ask, you must believe and not doubt, because the one who doubts is like a wave of the sea, blown and tossed by the wind. That person should not expect to*

receive anything from the Lord."
– James 1:6-7 (NIV)

You have Jesus praying and a great cloud of witnesses cheering you on to discover the great gift of faith that God has given you.

Transformers
When my son was young, he had a toy that would stand tall as a robot, but could also, with his assistance, transform into a vehicle. Movies were made of this superhero and many people flocked to theaters to watch these adventures. There is nothing like a good come-to-the-rescue movie.

You are a superhero. Yes. Perhaps not on your own, but with faith in God, you have the ability to speak the word and change your circumstances. I don't mean to just say a few words and wait. You have to be committed and interacting with God's word in your relationship with him.

> *"When someone has been given much, much will be required in return; and when someone has been entrusted with much, even more will*

be required."
– Luke 12:48 (NLT)

There are times when non-Christians or people just young in the faith will ask God for something. It appears that God will just allow them to do the minimal before he shows up with the answer. However, I believe there are also times when we have been walking with the Lord for so long that he requires more of us.

When you realize that God has truly given you the key to all the benefits he has for kingdom living, you will truly be in awe of our magnificent, almighty God. Faith is the currency of heaven. Any transaction you want to make with God requires faith.

I am stretching my faith now as I am believing for healing in my body. Nearly twenty years ago, a doctor diagnosed me with cancer. I was young then, but I knew Jesus and had a small measure of faith. It has been a journey, but I am still standing in joy and peace. This is a testimony itself, and for quite awhile, I camped out there.

As I continued to grow in the Lord, I felt he was encouraging me to believe for complete healing. As I studied, I realized that Jesus paid the price for my healing just as he did to take away my sins. The biggest leap for me in this phase was to realize that when I prayed for salvation, nothing noticeable happened that anyone could see. I simply prayed and believed by faith that I was saved. So, God moved me to pray for healing. At that moment, I did not notice any change, however, I simply believe by faith that I am healed.

Honestly, there is so much in the word concerning healing. I believe that you must seek God for his direction for you. But do know that God wants you to be well? He wants you to be whole.

So, let's activate the super power of faith in our lives by speaking only what is in agreement with the word of God. Whether you are waiting on answers concerning business, relationships, finances or healing, faith is your supernatural key to walk into your destiny.

"For we live by faith, not by sight."
– 2 Corinthians 5:7 (NIV)

Rise up and believe.

CHAPTER 3

Rise Up and Pray

Prayer is something I grew up seeing as a regular church attendee. As I recall, even when my mother listened to her favorite gospel radio show, it was interspersed with her own worship and prayers. I saw the deacons stand in front of the church and lead the congregation in a song of meditation and prayer. I have heard of the all-night prayer lock-ins. I have seen people pray in tongues from the pulpit, and I have seen those who seem to get louder and more dramatic as they continue to pray. I have seen people on their knees and lying on the altar, and those who simply prayed while sitting in their seat. Is there a right way to pray? Let's talk about it.

<u>What is Prayer?</u>
Prayer is communication with God. It sounds simple, but it is not as easy as you may think. Merriam-Webster defines communication as *"a process by which information is exchanged between individuals through a common system of symbols,*

signs, or behavior." One of the main ways we communicate is through speech.

I can recall being in China Town where people were speaking Mandarin. I tried communicating with one of the individuals and it was nearly impossible. I didn't understand the Mandarin language and he didn't understand the English language. No matter how much you talk and explain, if the other person doesn't understand, you haven't effectively communicated.

What relationship do you know that can be maintained without communication? When you meet someone new, it is not unusual to hold back information until you get to know them better. After you have spent a lot of time with them, you begin to trust them more and you open up and share more freely. It is imperative that we open up and pray to God. In doing so, we further develop our relationship with God. We come to know him more and our trust in him grows deeper.

<u>How to Pray</u>
Prayer is also an opportunity to have intimate time

with God. An acrostic that I learned many years ago is ACTS. Each letter stands for something you should address during your prayer time.

A – Adoration
C – Confession
T – Thanksgiving
S – Supplication

1. Adoration is the expression of deep love and respect as well as worship.[6] During this phase of prayer, you are just praising God for all of his wonderful attributes. Earlier, we talked about some of the names of God, which represent attributes that you can praise him for. You can praise him for nature and for anything good. You can speak it or you can use music and sing it.

I love worship songs that connect with my spirit. One song I like to listen to is *Still Believe* featuring Kim Walker-Smith. When I start praising God for his faithfulness, I begin to think of my own life situations and start applying the fact that God is faithful in my situation as well. If you haven't tried it before, try it the next time you're feeling down about something going on in your life. Put on a worship song and start singing along.

I remember being in a somber mood once. I turned on some worship and laid across the bed. By the end of one song, I was propped up on my elbow singing. A short time later, I was sitting up. And before it was over, I could feel God's presence. I was standing up with my arms lifted worshiping my all-powerful God. There is nothing like being in his presence. In his presence, all of our problems seem to shrink, because "greater is he that is in you, than he that is in the world" (1 John 4:4). Our issues don't just disappear, but in that intimate place, we begin to see them from a different perspective.

2. Confession is when we admit to God that we have missed the mark. We have sinned. Everyone has sinned at some point.

> *"If we say that we have no sin, we deceive ourselves, and the truth is not in us."*
> *– I John 1:8 (NIV)*

I believe that it is best to confess our sins daily and

even more often when we realize we have fallen short of God's expectation. Sin has a way of dulling our spiritual senses and hindering our fellowship and communication with God. It's best to get that roadblock out of the way as soon as possible.

> *"If we confess our sins, he is faithful and just to forgive us our sins, and to cleanse us from all unrighteousness."*
> *– I John 1:9 (NIV)*

3. Thanksgiving is something that God desires, but often does not get. Remember the story of the ten lepers in Luke 17:11-19 (NIV). Jesus was on his way to Jerusalem when he came upon ten lepers. They didn't come too close to him, but they called out in a loud voice, *"Jesus, Master, have pity on us!"*

Jesus told them to, *"Go, show yourselves to the priests."* Ten miracles happened as they went. They were all healed. When the Samaritan saw that he was healed, he went back to Jesus. He started praising and thanking him. Jesus said, *"Were not all ten cleansed? Where are the other nine? Has no one returned to give praise to God except this foreigner?"*

God wants us to be thankful. He wants us to, *"Give thanks in all circumstances; for this is God's will for you in Christ Jesus"* (I Thessalonians 5:18 NIV). Whatever state you find yourself in, it is an opportunity to give thanks. God is always at work behind the scene. Much of the time, we are not aware of what he is doing on our behalf, but we experience the benefits. We must give thanks and pray, believing that the answer to our circumstances is on the way.

His hope is that at some point, faith will arise in us and we will begin to thank God in advance for the things we have prayed for, because we know he is faithful. Trusting in him causes us to live in a state of expectancy. God wants us to look to him for our needs and desires.

> *"Delight thyself also in the Lord: and he shall give thee the desires of thine heart."*
> *– Psalms 37:4 (NIV)*

4. Supplication is the act of asking for something

earnestly and humbly. This prayer can be for you, your friends and family, in addition to your city, state, or country. If you are going to pray, you should be expecting an answer.

> *"Therefore, I tell you, whatever you ask for in prayer, believe that you have received it, and it will be yours."*
> *– Mark 11:24 (NIV)*

How are you asking? Are you just tossing your words in prayer into the atmosphere and hoping for the answer or are you asking, believing, and expecting? I don't like wasting time, and praying without believing sounds like a waste of time, energy and breath.

> *"If ye abide in me, and my words abide in you, ye shall ask what ye will, and it shall be done unto you."*
> *– John 15:7 (ESV)*

In this verse, you'll notice there are some stipulations concerning abiding. This is true of most of God's promises. He expects something of us.

> *"The one who keeps God's commands lives in him, and he in them. And this is how we know that he lives in us: We know it by the Spirit he gave us."*
> *– I John 3:24 (NIV)*

Abiding or living in him is his requirement to experience the best he has to offer.

> *"But my God shall supply all your need according to his riches in glory by Christ Jesus."*
> *– Philippians 4:19 (KJV)*

This scripture makes allowing God to call the shots in our lives all worth it. We can expect him to provide for us. Whatever we need, God's got it.

<u>Praying the Scriptures</u>
In Matthew, Jesus began telling us the dos and don'ts of prayer. Then, he tells us how to pray.

> *"After this manner therefore pray ye: Our*

Father which art in heaven, Hallowed be thy name. Thy kingdom come, Thy will be done in earth, as it is in heaven. Give us this day our daily bread. And forgive us our debts, as we forgive our debtors. And lead us not into temptation, but deliver us from evil: For thine is the kingdom, and the power, and the glory, forever. Amen."

– Matthew 6:9-13 (KJV)

It appears that we should start prayer by acknowledging Father God, and then giving him praise and worship. Next, we need to pray for God's kingdom to come. His will is done in his kingdom. And we want heaven on Earth literally. Heaven is a representation of God's perfect will. Whatever is okay in heaven is okay on Earth. Is what you're dealing with in heaven? If not, then it shouldn't be on Earth. Is sickness in heaven? No. Then it shouldn't be on Earth.

We also need to pray for what we will eat daily, as well as other needed provisions. Lastly, we cannot forget forgiveness. Living with unforgiveness is widely known to stop the flow of God's blessings, even when we are the ones who have been wronged. We need to pray to forgive. It may not be as much for the other person as it is for us. We should also pray that we will receive forgiveness.

Have you ever heard a family member of a victim speak up and say they forgive the offender for taking the life of their family member? I believe that people who do this are aware that living with unforgiveness is like drinking poison and waiting for the other person to die. Put forgiveness at the top of your list of things to work out in your heart.

Lastly, we need to pray that we don't fall into temptation and that we are delivered from evil. No matter how good we think we are, we can't keep ourselves. We have a deceitful enemy. We need to ask God to help us make the best choices to prevent us from falling into a trap.

You can pray any scripture by speaking the words as you are in touch with the heart of God. In doing so, your prayers are assured to be in God's will.

When to Pray

There is not a definite amount of time that God requires us to pray; in fact, he says to pray continually and without ceasing. I imagine that you are wondering *how in the world can I pray like that? I won't be able to get anything else done.* It's all in the way you look at it.

As various people or things come to your mind, pray for them. As you go about your day, you can pray for someone on your prayer list. You can pray for a task or project you're working on. You can pray for your church and your city. You can pray for favorable relationships on your job. The list can be never-ending. So, you don't have to stop what you are doing to have some kind of formal prayer. You simply pray as you go.

There are times when the Bible speaks of praying in the morning and in the evening. This is okay too. The most important thing is that we pray.

Where to Pray

"And when you pray, do not be like the hypocrites, for they love to pray standing in

> the synagogues and on the street corners to be seen by others. Truly I tell you, they have received their reward in full."
> – Matthew 6:5 (NIV)

This is interesting. I am sure every city has at least one street preacher. I believe that any time the word is going forth, it is making an impact on someone. However, I will say that it is important for them to get alone with God and continue to nurture their personal relationships with him.

> "But when you pray, go into your room, close the door and pray to your Father, who is unseen. Then your Father, who sees what is done in secret, will reward you."
> – Matthew 6:6 (NIV)

The movie *War Room* gave us a great idea of how to pray. In the movie, the main character removes most of her shoes and clothes from her closet to make room for her to go in and have a place to sit and pray. She even put up prayer requests on the walls of her closet.

If you want to create your own prayer closet, you might want to bring in a chair, your Bible, a notepad and pen, as well as your prayer requests. Make sure you have enough light to see, in addition to your reading glasses. It also doesn't have to be an actual closet. It may be a spare room or the corner of a room.

<u>Types of Prayer</u>
"...The prayer of a righteous person is powerful and effective."
– James 5:16 (NIV)

Prayer in Agreement
"Again, truly I tell you that if two of you on earth agree about anything they ask for, it will be done for them by my Father in heaven."
– Matthew 18:19-20 (NIV)

It is very important to have a prayer partner or a group of people you can choose from who understand the power of prayer as well as the power of agreement. Sometimes, people pray for whatever they want concerning a situation, however, it is more effective to focus all the prayers in agreement for more power. All the force directed to one point can speed up the time of breakthrough.

Prayer of Intercession

> *"I urge, then, first of all, that petitions, prayers, intercession and thanksgiving be made for all people— for kings and all those in authority, that we may live peaceful and quiet lives in all godliness and holiness."*
> *– I Timothy 2:1 (NIV)*

We are our brothers' keepers. When one of us is weak, another can help us persevere by praying. When I was sick in the hospital, it was hard for me to keep up my routine of saying specific prayers and quoting scriptures. Though I prayed and I know God heard me, it wasn't always as strategic as it was previously. That's where family and friends were able to cover me in prayer. I truly believe their prayers made a difference in my recovery.

Listening Prayer
It seems like a lot of people like to go in prayer and talk to God continually. This is certainly okay, but

we also need to listen. Sometimes, God wants to give us enough information to make a small change in our lives, a change that will make a huge difference in our lives.

Other times, God may want to speak to us and correct us when we are veering off track; this is to get us where we need to be.

If you want to hear from God, submit yourself to him and pray. After you're done, take some time to be quiet and reflect on what comes into your mind. Reading your Bible after praying is also a great way to listen.

Remember, God is omniscient. He knows everything. Whatever question you have, he has an answer. Rise up and pray. Then listen.

Chapter 4

Rise Up to Freedom

In my church, I've had the opportunity to participate as an attendee, as well as a leader in Freedom small groups. This study is certainly not the only way to experience personal breakthrough, but it is one that works for a lot of people. I think that every person could benefit from going through this class.

If you are having a difficult time assimilating the first three chapters of this book, it may be because something inside of you is hindering you from experiencing the abundant life that God has designed for you.

The Freedom curriculum gives people a safe place to engage God and the opportunity to explore our relationship with God in a way that often brings breakthrough and freedom when people least expect it. At the end of the class and especially after the conference, many people are changed for life.

Some want to lead a class. Others gained what they needed and are free to experience life in its fullness.

"So, if the Son sets you free, you will be free indeed."
– *John 8:36 (NIV)*

We become free in several ways, but especially from emotional baggage, past hurts, and the pain of not feeling good enough. Sometimes, we don't even know what's blocking us from becoming all God created us to be. Know it or not, the blockage has the power to stop us from reaching our destinies.

Mentoring
I read a story of a young lady who'd always wanted to go to graduate school. She took the GRE (Graduate School Exam) and didn't do well. She stopped pursuing that dream and satisfied herself with her career achievements in the field she was working in. She was doing very well, when one day, that old dream popped up again. but this time, she was ready. She went back to school, earned a Master's Degree and set an example for others who may think it's too late to go after their dreams.

When we enter or return to God's school, he leads us to *"throw off everything that hinders and the sin that so easily entangles"* (Hebrews 12:1). This is when we are able to hear and receive God's truth. This is where we begin to demolish the lies that we have believed. The more you engage in this process, the more you will experience freedom and momentum to run the race toward your destiny.

> *"No weapon that is formed against you will prosper."*
> *– Isaiah 54:17 (NASB)*

In the working world, mentors are often very busy and their time is valuable, so you should appreciate them, rather than waste their time. However, on the spiritual side of things, God is a mentor. He is omniscient, omnipotent, and omnipresent. He has unlimited time.

Who wouldn't want a mentor who is all-powerful on the streets and in the boardroom? He can make things happen. And how about a mentor who is everywhere at the same time, no matter the time zone? Last, but not least, a mentor who knows everything ought to be in high demand. No longer would you have to guess about someone's motives. Just ask your mentor.

There are definite benefits to having a real live person as your mentor, but never give up your spiritual mentor in God. You can always use a perfect opinion.

All We Need
The discussion of freedom often leads to the question, "What do we need to be free from?" The answer is simple and straightforward if we compare it to kidnapping and captivity. We need to be free from whoever or whatever is holding us in bondage. I sometimes think of what it must have been like for the three ladies held captive by a man in Cleveland. After being abducted as teenagers and a young adult, they lived about ten years of their lives being physically, sexually, and emotionally abused. Thinking about them makes me realize how many of us are free to roam as we please, but are still held captive by the strongholds in our minds. There is often some lie that we believe that causes us to get stuck in life or not accomplish all we are capable of

accomplishing. One lady admitted that because her daddy left her as a child, she didn't think she deserved any better, so she allowed the males she was in relationship with to abuse her.

Let's put in the work to discover any lies we are believing, so we can keep moving toward the destiny God has for us. Celebrate Recovery, another biblically based program, addresses "hurt, hang-ups, and habits." Here and now, we will identify bondages as hurts, hang-ups, and bad habits.

> *"His divine power has given us everything we need for a godly life through our knowledge of him who called us by his own glory and goodness. Through these he has given us his very great and precious promises, so that through them you may participate in the divine nature, having escaped the corruption in the world caused by evil desires."*
> *– 2 Peter 1:3-4 (NIV)*

So, if you believe in God and his word, you can stand tall knowing that whatever you are facing, God's power has given you everything you need to live a godly life.

We become aware of the things we need as we grow in our knowledge of God. We get to know him through our relationship with his Son. When we see the Son, we see God. He is the exact image of the Father and only does what the Father does. When you spend enough time with people on a regular basis, you get to know their character. The same is true when we spend time with Jesus. He is a perfect representation of God.

Over the years, I have watched my sons play video games. Some of the games are easy, but as they have gotten older, they have played more complex games. I am not as good as they are at playing, but I've noticed many of the games seem to have some things in common. The player's goal is to complete a specific course to win the game. However, when you complete that course, you realize that there is another level that's more challenging than the previous one. This happens repeatedly until the player reaches the ultimate goal of successfully completing each level of the game. This goal is often completed over time. How fast the player completes the game depends on the time he or she commits to playing, as well as how long it takes the player to maneuver through the obstacle courses and overcome the obstacles that try to prevent his/her success. There must be a strategy involved to overcome. Often, the player has an opportunity to access more power to help him or her confront every enemy and obstacle that stands in his or her way. This sounds a lot like life.

We move to higher levels in our relationships with God as we continue to get to know him and his ways. When we are successful at one thing, we don't pack up and wait for our heavenly wings. No. There is more. As we face new challenges, God is the only one to judge and determine if we have successfully utilized the things that he has given us. If so, we move on to the next level and a different challenge. One of the popular adages of today is: *new level, new devil*. We win as we access and participate in the divine nature of God and move from glory to glory.

Free to Soar
"So, if the Son sets you free, you will be free

indeed."

– John 8:36 (NIV)

Know this. God wants you to soar. He doesn't want you to be like the eagle that thought it was a chicken. Read the story below.

> A baby eagle became orphaned when something happened to his parents. He glided down to the ground from his nest, but was not yet able to fly. A man picked him up. The man took him to a farmer and said, "This is a special kind of barnyard chicken that will grow up big." The farmer said, "Don't look like no barnyard chicken to me." "Oh yes, it is. You will be glad to own it." The farmer took the baby eagle and placed it with his chickens.
>
> The baby eagle learned to imitate the chickens. He could scratch the ground for grubs and worms too. He grew up thinking he was a chicken.
>
> One day, an eagle flew over the barnyard.

The eagle looked up and wondered, "What kind of animal is that? How graceful, powerful, and free it is." He then asked another chicken, "What is that?" The chicken replied, "Oh, that is an eagle. But don't worry yourself about that. You will never be able to fly like that."

And the eagle went back to scratching the ground. He continued to behave like the chicken he thought he was. Finally, he died never knowing the grand life that could have been his.

Do you see yourself as a barnyard chicken? Are you oblivious to your own strengths and abilities? How would it feel to soar like an eagle in your personal and professional life? I have wasted some time, but I am determined not to go to my grave without exploring the vast abilities and opportunities that God has availed to me. What about you? Let go of what's holding you back and rise up to freedom.

Potential
I am excited about the book *No Limits* by John C.

Maxwell. He says, "If you grow in your awareness, develop your abilities, and make the right choices, you can reach your capacity." And he has an equation; it is:

AWARENESS + ABILITY + CHOICES = CAPACITY

Maxwell suggests that awareness is important. "If you don't know what's limiting you, how can you overcome it?" he asks.

Next, we have our abilities. We each have a unique set of things we are good at, all on various levels. We have a combination of strengths and weaknesses. We are all gifted at something. I personally see capacity as our potential.

Lastly, our choices can turn the ship of our lives toward success or failure. Oftentimes, we can recover from some choices as if we'd simply taken a detour in life. There are other times where our choices can have lifelong consequences attached to them. So, let's talk to Father God and seek his advice before making decisions. I have a bracelet and a shirt that has "Pray First" printed on them.

Sometimes, these can be subtle reminders that make a world of difference.

Scientists have discovered there are untapped diamonds in Antarctica, meaning no one has mined the area to retrieve the jewels. If they are right, there are riches lying under the surface of that continent. The potential is there for people to retrieve these diamonds and become wealthy. Maybe God is calling you to tap into the abilities he's given you. Maybe he wants you to get involved in some task or assignment that could catapult you to success.

It turns out that the U.S. and other countries put a fifty year hold on any mining expeditions in that area of Antarctica. It won't be lifted until 2041. In this instance, the untapped potential of the diamonds are legally required to remain hidden. What is lying just beneath your surface? Jim Rohn says, "There lies within each person a huge reservoir of untapped potential for achievement, success, happiness." What are you waiting for? There is no law requiring you to remain as you are. Explore your talents and abilities and rise.

In His Presence

Let's do what it takes to use this freedom that we have to soar. The meaning of freedom, according to Google Dictionary, is: *"the power or right to act, speak, or think as one wants without hindrance or restraint."* Remember, the freedom we speak of has boundaries. Because Jesus set us free, we are free from whatever it was that enslaved us. Now that you are free, you can say no to whatever you couldn't say no to before. Accept it by faith.

> *"Now the Lord is the Spirit, and where the Spirit of the Lord is, there is freedom."*
> – 2 Corinthians 3:17 (NIV)

It is important to spend time with Jesus. In the Lord's presence, everything that seems to be an obstacle to you will seem smaller compared to Almighty God. You see, as you go about your day, you'll hear thoughts from the enemy telling you that your godly perspective isn't real. You can't expect God to get you out of this situation. This is when you have to discern who is speaking to you and who you are going to listen to. God's word says that all things are possible with him. That's right. All things.

We can't pick and choose what we want to believe if we are all in with God. We have to believe the whole Bible.

It is true that we have a better covenant in the New Testament, but:

> "All Scripture is God-breathed and is useful for teaching, rebuking, correcting and training in righteousness, so that the servant of God may be thoroughly equipped for every good work."
> – Timothy 3:16-17 (NIV)

Being in God's presence allows us to hear him speaking to us without distractions. If you are open, that's the time God can give you supernatural insights. He can also correct you to make sure you are on the right path. Training in righteousness is definitely something that we need to rise up to freedom, because we want to get and maintain access to all of the benefits God offers to his children.

Let's look at two kinds of righteousness. One is self-righteousness, which is based on you doing good works and obeying the law. That type of righteousness can really leave you in a bind, because there will be times when you miss the mark.

The God kind of righteousness is yours, not because you have been good and done things right, but it is available to you just because of your relationship with Christ Jesus.

> *"God made him who had no sin to be sin for us, so that in him we might become the righteousness of God."*
> *– 2 Corinthians 5:21 (NIV)*

Jesus took our sins upon himself as he was nailed to the cross. Now, we have the opportunity to live in him; we can now filter how we see, think and act through the lens of scripture and thereby, be the righteousness of God.

> *"It is because of him that you are in Christ Jesus, who has become for us wisdom from God—that is, our righteousness, holiness and*

redemption."

– I Corinthians 1:30 (NIV)

Because we are in Christ, we have access to wisdom and righteousness. As long as we are in Christ, we are righteous. It's not about what we do or don't do. It is about our position in Christ. So, when you mess up, it doesn't jeopardize your righteousness as long as you confess your sins and remain in Christ.

The truth is, the times you mess up should be decreasing as you spend more time in Christ. You have been saved from sin; you can now say no to it. Before you were saved, you didn't have the power to say no and follow through. Now that you are saved, you must spend time in the word and in God's presence until you accept and believe that you are free.

> *"No temptation has overtaken you except what is common to mankind. And God is faithful; he will not let you be tempted beyond what you can bear. But when you are tempted, he will also provide a way out so that you can endure it."*

– I Corinthians 10:13 (NIV)

The next time you are faced with a temptation, ask God where the way out is and look for it. He will reveal it to you. From there, it will be your choice to take the way of escape. That is how you rise above temptation to freedom. Each time you make the God choice, you soar a little higher.

Chapter 5

Rise Up in Peace

"You will keep in perfect peace those whose minds are steadfast, because they trust in you."
— *Isaiah 26:3 (NIV)*

I stood at the edge of the Canadian bank overlooking the Niagara river. Surprisingly, where I stood, there was no railing to prevent someone from just walking into the water. Now that I think about it, it would probably be very expensive to try to fence off the sides of every river. But this was just a few feet from Niagara Falls.

The water was clear as it moved steadily toward the falls. I thought perhaps it was moving much swifter than my eyes acknowledged. That's when I noticed the rocks. They were very large and looked almost like tiny islands. A few sea gulls were walking on the rocks and they seemed quite comfortable. I, however, was becoming increasingly uneasy about being so close to the falls without a rail to prevent me from accidentally ending up in the water.

Several yards away, the most powerful waterfall I'd ever seen was ready to hurl anything or anybody over the falls for a 165 foot drop, followed by several tons of water. The thought was enough to make me take a few steps back from the bank.

What touched me was the way the sea gulls seemed oblivious to what lay a few yards away. They felt safe on the rock. Now, that's peace.

The Rock

How do you react when there is danger lurking near you? Are you able to carry on like the sea gulls, as if there is nothing to worry about? Well, this should be our goal. I am better about it now, but there was a time when I could hear some bad news, and I would start thinking about all the possible negative outcomes that could affect me or my family. God does not want that for us.

> *"Don't worry about anything; instead, pray about everything. Tell God what you need,*

> *and thank him for all he has done. Then you will experience God's peace, which exceeds anything we can understand. His peace will guard your hearts and minds as you live in Christ Jesus."*
> – *Philippians 4:6-7 (NLT)*

So, exactly where does worry fit into a Christian's life? It's like taking a piece from a farm puzzle and trying to fit it in to an aquarium puzzle. It won't fit. Worry does not belong in our lives. God wants us to come to him for whatever we need, whether it be a physical or emotional need. He wants to be our Rock.

We need to talk to God about what we need and thank him for who he is and all he's done. This is the pathway to experiencing a level of peace that most people just can't understand. This peace will shield your heart and your mind from all the negative thoughts and words that you may hear.

> *"Keep thy heart with all diligence; for out of it are the issues of life."*
> – *Proverbs 4:23 (KJV)*

Ideas and thoughts can easily get into your heart through your eyes and ears. You must be diligent about blocking out the bad influences.

Be a Thermostat

Are you a thermometer or a thermostat? A thermometer reads the temperature of its surroundings, but a thermostat sets the temperature of its surroundings. If you are on your job and your coworker comes in melancholy, your boss is angry, or a colleague is critical, what do you do? Is your attitude affected by theirs? Do you find yourself getting melancholy, angry or critical? That's an example of being a thermometer. However, if you are able to maintain your peaceful attitude, you are making the choice as to how things will go in your own space, regardless of what others do. That's an example of a thermostat.

You can decide before you leave home that, no matter what happens, I am going to be peaceful today. It's harder, though not impossible, if you wait until the moment something negative happens to do this. The goal is to set the thermostat at peace and leave it there.

This is hard to do if you're not spending some quality time in God's presence. He is peace, and when you take time to bask in his presence, that same peace will be imparted to you. If you aren't sure how to do this, here are a couple of pointers. Turn on some worship music that basically sings about how great God is. Sing along. Tell God how much you love him. Pray and ask God to reveal himself to you. Meditate on scripture. Repeat it several times. Think about how you can use the scripture in your everyday life. Now, you're ready to set the temperature for those around you.

Remember, Moses came down from the mountain after being in the presence of God and his face was radiant. It is possible that people may notice something different about you when you have been hanging out with Father God. It's also possible that some may not realize exactly what is different about you, even though they'll sense a change.

God's Peace
According to Google's dictionary, the definition of peace is *"freedom from disturbance; quiet and tranquility"* and *"freedom from or the cessation of*

war or violence."

By this definition, the only way to have peace is to prevent disturbance and violence from occurring around you, and to have tranquil silence. This sounds good, but for most of us, it is not practical. When you're dealing with people, especially children, they are not always going to get along.

There will likely be some type of discord or disturbance to rise up. Many of us live in cities where crime is prevalent. Does it bother you when the news reporters talk about sexual harassment, property break-ins, or shootings? Can you still sleep well?

With all the things that go on in the world today, I don't think we'd ever have peace if we had to depend on the dictionary's definition of peace. Instead, God says:
> *"Peace I leave with you; my peace I give you. I do not give to you as the world gives. Do not let your hearts be troubled and do not be afraid."*
> *– John 14:27 (NIV)*

In this verse, God promises us that he leaves us his peace. He just gives it to us, but it's different from what the world gives. That's the dictionary's definition of peace and it doesn't have the power that God's peace has.

God gives us a peace that surpasses understanding. He gives us the kind of peace that causes us not to worry, even when we're in the midst of of turmoil or crime. In fact, he tells us not to let our hearts be troubled and do not be afraid. So, if we trust God and act on his word, we can go on to sleep believing that all will be well.

> *"In peace I will lie down and sleep, for you alone, LORD, make me dwell in safety."*
> *– Psalm 4:8 (NIV)*

There may be times you can't sleep, but it should never be due to worry or fear. We must trust God.

Authority

God tells us, *"I urge, then,...that petitions, prayers, intercession and thanksgiving be made for all people —for kings and all those in authority, that we may live peaceful and quiet lives in all godliness and holiness."*

– 1 Timothy 2:1-2 (NIV)

Let me just say that if we are going to rise up to peace, we must also make a concerted effort to pray for our elected officials, officers of the law and anyone in authority. God said to pray "for kings and all those in authority, that we may live peaceful and quiet lives in all godliness and holiness" (I Timothy 2:2 NIV).

Truth be told, those who are in authority are people, just like us, and all people have their shortcomings and room to grow. Those who are in authority are likely to have more responsibility than the average person, all the while bearing the high expectations many people have for them.

Lean toward giving people the benefit of the doubt, pray for them and expect God to do something amazing in their lives. This could result in their behavior becoming more pleasing to God and more palatable for mankind. If these people in authority make bad choices, let's pray for them. If they are close to you, walk beside and encourage them until they get on the right track.

None of us want to be beat up with words when we mess up. So, let's treat people the way we want to be treated. It could be a child, a friend, a husband or someone else. The truth is that if you are focused on talking badly about someone, you will give off bad energy, hinder your relationship with God and make it difficult for you to remain in a state of peace.

> *"If it is possible, as far as it depends on you, live at peace with everyone."*
> *– Romans 12:18 (NIV)*

We are responsible to do what we can to live at peace with people. It will be hard to do if your mouth is always ready to speak negatively about someone. Rise above critical talk.

When Big Brother Leaves

> *"I have told you these things, so that in me you may have peace. In this world you will have trouble. But take heart! I have overcome the world."*

– John 16:33 (NIV)

Chapter 16 of the Book of John contains warnings about the troubles the disciples would face once Jesus went back to the Father. This book also contains comforting promises like Jesus saying he would visit them after the resurrection.

For the disciples, it was Jesus, their big brother, who was leaving them. I tried to imagine how the disciples received this message. I am sure they understood the gravity of the situation, just by the tone and speech Jesus had given them. But could they really grasp what he was talking about and what it would mean to them and humanity?

> *"Both the one who makes people holy and those who are made holy are of the same family. So, Jesus is not ashamed to call them brothers and sisters."*
>
> *– Hebrew 2:11 (NIV)*

According to this scripture, we are brothers and sisters of Jesus. After all, God gave us the right to become children of God and Jesus is God's firstborn.

So, we are all in the family. I imagine that having a big brother can be beneficial at times. Perhaps, you need understanding about something you've heard, protection from bullies, or to know that someone besides your mother and your father cares about you. If Jesus was walking in the flesh beside me every day, showing me how to do ministry and how to love all people, I would not want him to leave. Jesus had such compassion that he had the disciples to sit down as he poured out his heart, telling them what to expect, so they wouldn't be at a loss once he was taken into custody and crucified.

I believe that though Jesus is seated in heaven, he still has that same compassion for us. If we will take the time to worship and pray, I'm sure Jesus would begin to speak to us and tell us great and wonderful things we don't know.

With the disciples, Jesus never sugarcoated the truth. He told them, in this world you're going to have trouble. Think about it. There are people who come to Jesus believing that they will never have another problem. Somewhere during the witnessing stage, they either assumed this or it was implied. The trouble with this thinking is that when trouble comes, these new converts are ready to give up, but if we talk to them with compassion and are upfront with them, they'll be prepared to stand. Jesus also told us not to worry because he has overcome the world.

<u>In Jesus</u>
Most of the scriptures somehow state or imply that this peace is in Jesus, and if you're in him, you have access to this peace.

> *"Abide in me, and I in you. As the branch cannot bear fruit of itself, except it abide in the vine; no more can ye, except ye abide in me."*
>
> *– John 15:4 (KJV)*

> *"Remain in me, as I also remain in you. No branch can bear fruit by itself; it must remain in the vine. Neither can you bear fruit unless you remain in me."*
>
> *– John 15:4 (NIV)*

—

I have taken a scripture with two different versions

to talk about. Abide. I like that old King James Version word. It means to dwell, to continue, to reside. This makes me think of "living in."

As I read the NIV, I see the word abide translated as remain. So, if I remain in Christ Jesus, live in him, and he remains in me, I have the ability to exude peace, because Jesus Christ is peace. Now, if we want this peace, we'd better figure out what it means to remain in him.

Jesus declared himself as, *"the living bread that came down from heaven. Whoever eats this bread will live forever. This bread is my flesh."*
– John 6:51 (NIV)

In John 6:56, he states that, *"Whoever eats my flesh and drinks my blood remains in me, and I in them."(NIV)* So now, we know the requirement to remain in him.

When we take communion, we are at that time eating the bread that represents Christ's body and drinking the wine that represents Jesus' blood. Every time we eat the bread (his body), we should remember that his body was broken for us to experience healing. He took the stripes so that we could walk in wholeness. When we drink the wine (the blood), we should remember that through the shedding of his blood, Jesus bore our sins; he took them away from us. We are now free from sin; it is no longer our master.

Whenever you confess scripture and stand on God's word, you're feeding on the bread and thereby remaining in him and him in you. The same goes for every time you plead the blood of Jesus over yourself and loved ones, as well as every time you confess that the blood covers your sins and others' sin, shame and guilt.

You don't have to worry or fret about the bad choices you made in the past. They are now under the blood.

Take a black pen and write down all the sins that come to mind immediately. When you are done, take a red marker and make a big X over your paper. When you choose to believe in Jesus, all those sins are under the blood. You have been set free.

Rise Up in Peace

We can rise up in peace, because sin no longer has a hold on us. By faith, we accept that we are free, free to say no to sin and yes to righteousness.

Chapter 6

Rise Up on Purpose

A young man who I'll call Cedric used to get in trouble in high school for hanging with the wrong crowd. He did not have a plan for exactly what he would do when he graduated, but he assumed it would all work out. Then one day, he met a man who worked in an office. They chatted and seemed to make a connection. It turned into a regular meeting through which the gentleman was able to mentor Cedric. Eventually, Cedric graduated, stayed on the right path, got a full-time job, and graduated from a Christian college. For Cedric, that meeting was a rendezvous with purpose. The gentleman who mentored the young man was operating in his own purpose. The young man needed to identify his purpose before he became a statistic on the streets. Today, he is mentoring other young men. He has found his purpose. When you find purpose, it drives your life in the direction of destiny.

Firm Foundation

Think of a house of cards. You stand up cards next to each other and balance them to make walls. Then you take more cards and lay them a certain way to make the roof. Next, you begin to build on top of the standing cards. You may build a few levels, but at some point, the house of cards will likely tumble down, because the foundation was not firm.

Whenever you are going to construct a building, it needs to be on a firm foundation or you could end up with major problems. People often discover an issue with the foundation when they see cracks in the walls, or when doors and windows will no longer close the way they used to. These issues usually arise when the building site was not properly prepared, or the soil wasn't stabilized. It could be due to a contractor wanting to cut corners on materials or performance, or it could be due to a lack of knowledge on the contractor's part.

> *"Anyone who listens to my teaching and follows it is wise, like a person who builds a house on solid rock. Though the rain comes in torrents and the floodwaters rise and the*

winds beat against that house, it won't collapse because it is built on bedrock. But anyone who hears my teaching and doesn't obey it is foolish, like a person who builds a house on sand. When the rains and floods come and the winds beat against that house, it will collapse with a mighty crash."
– Matthew 7:24-27 (NLT)

Lack of knowledge can be a game changer in the worst way. Hosea 4:6 (KJV) says, *"My people are destroyed for lack of knowledge."* It behooves us to know the foundation we are building on when constructing our lives or we could lose a lot.

Your foundation for building your life could include what your family thinks you should do. It could also include all that you have researched and set your goals to work toward. You have a plan. The issue is whether or not it is God's plan.

"For I know the plans I have for you," says the Lord. "They are plans for good and not for disaster, to give you a future and a hope."
– Jeremiah 29:11 (NLT)

God has a plan and you have a plan. You need to put them side by side and see if God's plan matches your plan. If not, you have a decision to make. It's a decision that could determine your destiny. No matter how great your five-year life plan sounds, if it isn't God's plan, you risk forfeiting your divine destiny if you follow it. You could have a successful career by the world's standard, but you could find yourself unfulfilled in your walk with God.

> *"People may spend their whole lives climbing the ladder of success only to find, once they reach the top, that the ladder is leaning against the wrong wall."*
> *– Stephen Covey*

If you love the Lord, then please consider seeking his direction for your purpose. It may not be possible to live life without any regrets, but before investing years pursuing a goal that isn't God's best for you, check it out with him.

Be aware that there are times when God will shake your foundations. He may be trying to dislodge any of those ideas and goals that you are so attached to that you can't see him or his plan for you.

God knows the right wall for you to climb.

Cornerstone

Once we've prepared our foundations and it's time to build, we can line up our walls against the cornerstone.

> *"Therefore, this is what the Sovereign LORD says: "Look! I am placing a foundation stone in Jerusalem, a firm and tested stone. It is a precious cornerstone that is safe to build on. Whoever believes need never be shaken."*
> *– Isaiah 28:16 (NLT)*

> *"Jesus is 'the stone you builders rejected, which has become the cornerstone.'"*
> *– Acts 4:11 (NIV)*

In these scriptures, we see that the cornerstone is a metaphor for Jesus. Jesus was rejected and crucified, but he arose. This is why whoever believes in him doesn't have to be shaken, no matter what is happening in his or her life. Jesus is a firm foundation.

Jesus wants to be the cornerstone of your goal setting for your future. He wants you to come to him to talk over what you want to do.

> *"Commit to the LORD whatever you do, and he will establish your plans."*
> *– Proverbs 16:3 (NIV)*

There is nothing better than having the Lord's seal of approval.

Glorifying God

What is our purpose as human beings? I believe our purpose in general is to glorify God, but how exactly do we do that? We can praise him, express our admiration of him, and show our respect and gratitude. We can worship him, offering him our adoration, reverence and obedience.

> *"Therefore, I urge you, brothers and sisters, in view of God's mercy, to offer your bodies as a living sacrifice, holy and pleasing to God—this is your true and proper worship."*

— *Romans 12:1 (NIV)*

When we offer our bodies, we offer our mouths, hands, eyes and every other part of our bodies as a sacrifice. We're alive, so it's a living sacrifice. We want our bodies to be holy and pleasing to God. When you want to give someone "a piece of your mind," choose to remain silent or speak a kind word instead. When your eyes see something that tempts you, the best thing to do is remove yourself from the situation. If your hands are abusing someone, stop. Every act of obedience is worship to God.

> *"...let your light shine before others, that they may see your good deeds and glorify your Father in heaven."*
> — *Matthew 5:16 (NIV)*

God is glorified when something you say or do influences others to give him glory.

> *"I glorified You on the earth, having accomplished the work which You have given Me to do.*
> — *John 17:4 (ESV)*

Finally, one way to glorify God is to accomplish the work he's given you to do. For me, the work includes writing this book. I have been talking about writing and publishing a book for a while, but I have always let life get in the way. I've written devotionals, articles, and blog posts, but not a book. In the back of my mind, I kept thinking that those things are good, but they are not what God is asking me to do. This time, God provided the time and gave me the grace to push through the process. During the difficult times, I could always think of the people who would likely read this book and how it might benefit them.

Nothing compares to being in God's perfect will ... his good, pleasing and perfect will. I always say that there are good things and God things. All of them may be good things to do, but maybe only one of them is the God thing for you.

> *"Many are the plans in a person's heart,*
> *but it is the Lord's purpose that prevails."*
> *– Proverbs 19:21 (NIV)*

I don't believe we get any points for doing a ton of

great things and overlooking the one thing that God has assigned to us. After all, God desires obedience, not sacrifice. It may not be anything that we think of as an awesome project, but to God, it is very important for us to follow through. God may just want us to stand up for someone who is being mistreated. He may just want us to forego taking up for ourselves in a situation and trust him to handle it. Each of these acts of obedience brings glory to God.

Necessity of Purpose
As believers, our main purpose in life is to glorify God. We do this by using our gifts and abilities to accomplish our purpose. Living in purpose is the path to our destiny. Why do we need to have a purpose? After all, we could just live each day as it comes. Below, I share a few benefits of knowing your purpose.

Purpose is where life begins.
Many of us just meander through life until we discover our purpose. One problem with this is that we waste a lot of time and leave reaching our destiny to fate. Having a life of purpose helps us

efficiently choose our goals and the actions we need to accomplish them. It's how we begin to live our lives on purpose. Start your search for purpose by thinking about the things that you value. How can you make a difference?

To do or not to do.
Having a life purpose allows us to distinguish between things we should or should not invest our time, energy, and money in. If the event, project, or purchase is in line with our purpose, we have a green light do it.

Fulfillment.
When you operate your life from purpose, your choices and actions are in line with the values you have. When you have reached your goals, you will feel a deep satisfaction knowing that you have achieved something that's in line with your goals and values. When people operate apart from their values, they eventually experience conflict within themselves. This can lead to a multitude of issues for the individual as well as their relationships.

Passion.

When you have a passion for what you are doing, you can work longer and harder, even while you're waiting on rewards.

> *"If you do what you love, you'll never work a day in your life."*
> – Marc Anthony

It really doesn't seem like work when you love what you're doing.

> *"Paul and I, we never thought that we would make much money out of the thing. We just loved writing software."*
> – Bill Gates

Who knows what will happen once you devote yourself to your life's purpose, doing what you love to do? And if you feel like you wasted time, read this:

> *"And we know that God causes everything to work together for the good of those who love God and are called according to his purpose*

for them."

– Romans 8:28 (NLT)

When you love God and are called according to his purpose, he will use whatever has happened in your life for good. Everything. Go ahead and get with God in prayer and allow him to speak to you about your purpose. After all, he created you. When he speaks, take hold of your purpose, write it down and run with it.

<u>Purpose</u>
We have done a lot of talking about purpose, but just what is purpose? Let's look at the definition from Dictionary.com. Purpose is "the reason for which something exists or is done, made, used, etc." The second definition is "an intended or desired result; end; aim; goal."
To simplify this, purpose is the reason you exist. It is also the intended result or the end you expect in your lifetime.

Purpose is one of those intangibles that we really should pursue. It is somehow intrinsically connected to who we are. Purpose is the path we use to get to the "expected end" God has planned for us.

> *"For I know the thoughts that I think toward you, saith the LORD, thoughts of peace, and not of evil, to give you an expected end."*
> *– Jeremiah 29:11 (KJV)*

God sees the big picture and he knows how each of us fits into it.

What the Stats Say

If you have already discovered your purpose, you are ahead of most of the world. According to the Gallup-Healthways Global Well-Being Index, "only 18% of the world's population has a thriving sense of purpose."

A report published in Psychosomatic Medicine: Journal of Biobehavioral Medicine, "found a substantive correlation between a higher sense of life purpose and a lower incidence of cardiovascular disease." The same study "found that a high sense of purpose resulted in a significantly lower overall risk of death."[6]

In another study, researchers reviewed over 6000 forms of questions and answers that people had completed. They reviewed the responses to questions and determined that, "people with a sense of purpose had a 15 percent lower risk of death, compared with those who said they were more or less aimless. And it didn't seem to matter the age when people found their direction. It could be in their 20s, 50s or 70s."[7]

Pertaining to the Alzheimer's disease, a recent study indicated that "participants who reported higher levels of purpose in life exhibited better cognitive function despite the burden of the disease."[8]

"Your outlook—having a sense of optimism and purpose—seems to be predictive of health outcomes," says Dr. Laura Kubzansky, professor of social and behavioral sciences at Harvard T.H. Chan School of Public Health.[9]

This information certainly suggests that it is beneficial to your health and well-being to have a purpose in life. If you are not one of the 18% of people in the world who have discovered your purpose, these study results should give you the motivation you need to rise up and pursue it.

CHAPTER 7

Rise Up to Identity

A few years ago, I was reviewing my bank statement when I noticed charges that I did not recognize. I called the bank and they began an investigation. I'm still not certain how thieves got my bank card number, but they started a shopping spree as if it was their own card. Apparently, they made a new card with my number. They were physically going into stores and making purchases in a different state with a card that had my information on it. They were forging my signature. Fortunately, before they could do too much damage, their actions were discovered. My bank covered the fraudulent charges. Although I suffered no financial loss, it was an inconvenience to have to deal with the situation and just a bit disconcerting to have someone electronically steal my identity.

<u>Living Supernaturally</u>
I have decided in some respects to take on the persona of superwoman. I'm still thinking about

whether or not to wear a cape. She is a fictional character or maybe multiple characters as seen in DC Comics. I believe we have something in common. She has super powers like super strength, super speed, flight, heat vision, and healing.

I believe that as a believer in Christ Jesus, I have access to a supernatural life.

> "...he has given us his very great and precious promises, so that through them you may participate in the divine nature...."
> – 2 Peter 1:4 (NIV)

The promises are the key. He gave us his promises and it is important what we do with them, whether we believe them or not, live by them, or act in regards to them. Believing the promises of God with an unwavering heart will unlock the divine nature, a way of living that often conflicts with the world, but allows us to experience an abundance of joy, peace, love, healing, and deliverance, among other things.

In 2003, Renee Napier lost her 20 year-old daughter when Eric Smallridge crashed into her car killing Meagan and her friend. According to CBS News, Renee was initially angry with Eric, but eventually found it in her heart to forgive him. She said, "In my opinion, forgiveness is the only way to heal." Renee went on to start a foundation in honor of her daughter and she and Eric often did speaking engagements together to warn teenagers of the dangers of drunk driving.[10]

That kind of forgiveness, in my opinion, is not natural. It is super-natural. The world would agree that she had every right to hate him and never forgive him. It took something above the natural way of thinking and believing for her to forgive him and subsequently work with him to help others. It took strength and peace beyond understanding.

I believe Jesus gives us this supernatural ability, as well as the ability to have peace in the midst of chaos and to love people who have mistreated us. But we must be aware of the fact that we have to choose to activate this ability. Many of the gifts of God lie dormant because people are expecting God to do all the work. When Jesus went to the cross and arose, he did his part ... all of it. There is nothing else that he needs to do. Imagine a farmer who wants a crop of corn. He can pray about it and he can wait, but if he never plants the seed, it is unlikely that he will see any corn grow.

Just as Superwoman's character could take flight, trusting in the word of God allows us to rise above the troubles in our lives.

> *"And God raised us up with Christ and seated us with him in the heavenly realms in Christ Jesus."*
>
> *– Ephesians 2:6 (NIV)*

I once visited the CNN Tower. From over eleven hundred feet up, my perspective was very different as I looked at cars on the ground. It seemed as if they were smaller than my finger. Likewise, when we look down on our problems from the heavenly realm, they no longer seem insurmountable. Lastly, I want to mention that Superwoman had the ability to heal wounds and diseases. I am sure that you have heard that Jesus took a brutal beating, and by his wounds, we are healed. Not only does he have the ability to heal, he has already paid the price for our healing. Now, it's just a matter of activating it in our bodies and the bodies of others. After all Jesus said, *"...whoever believes in me will do the works I have been doing, and they will do even greater things..."*

– John 14:12 (NIV)

As you can see, having a Superwoman persona is not all that unreasonable, but I think I will just be me, living and operating in the divine nature of God. This allows him to put his super on my natural, and I can rise up in my identity in Christ.

Who's Your Daddy?

When my husband was growing up and occasionally as an adult, people would see him and say, "That's one of those Woods." Woods is his surname and a lot of people addressed him and his siblings by it.

Having a recognized surname often prompts the question, "Are you related to ...?" Imagine if you met someone with the last name Obama. You might immediately ask them if they are related to Barak and Michelle Obama. If you were related to the

Obamas and shared their last name, you would probably have taken a visit to the White House. Their children, Malia and Sasha, had the opportunity to go into the private quarters anytime they wanted to because of who their daddy is. They could crawl around his office floor or sit next to him on the family sofa.

What benefits do you have because of your Father God? He allowed his son to shed his blood and die on the cross for our sins. By faith, we have been cleared of a legal debt. We deserved to be punished for our sins. We are now righteous. By his stripes, we are healed.

He is ready to back up his word and fulfill his promises. But how are we living? Are we living in our old identities, the people we once were before we accepted Christ as our Savior? Or have we believed that we are who the word of God says we are?

If you listen to the enemy's propaganda, he will present a case to you as to why you shouldn't even love yourself. He will bring up your past and every wrong thought you had or choice you made. But that was then, and this is now. If you are a believer, it's time to believe that you are a new creature. The old has become new.

> *"You have to be willing to let go of an old identity to take on a new identity."*
> *– Mark Batterson*

Because of who your daddy is, you have access to unimaginable benefits. "Learn from me," he says. Why do we ask our friends, when we could just ask Father God? Think about it; we have access to the mind of Christ.

Mistaken Identity

Mr. Ronald Cotton knows well the havoc that mistaken identity can bring to a life. According to innocenceproject.org, he served "ten years in prison for crimes he did not commit. His convictions were based largely on an eyewitness misidentification made by one of the victims."

After DNA testing, the court determined that Mr. Cotton was not guilty of the crime. The State Bureau of Investigation's DNA database showed a match with an inmate who had bragged to another inmate that he was the one who had committed the crime. He later plead guilty to the charges.

It is reasonable to see the similarity of this in our spiritual lives. We can be going about our daily lives believing a lie. Let's just say we have accepted a lie that we could never accomplish a certain thing. There will always be a voice ready to remind us of this lie, coaxing us into a life of mistaken identity.

Whenever we hear something that inspires us, and we garner a bit of courage to step out, the dream killer's voice awakens. That voice speaks up and says things like, "You can't. You're not ready. Somebody else could succeed, but not you." This is the moment that you must make a choice. You either choose to persevere, ignoring the voice and living your true identity, or you can silently agree with the voice, put your dream on a shelf and live out another identity. This is what happened to me. As I mentioned earlier, for years, I felt like I should write a book. There were always plenty of excuses why I could not or should not at the time. The bottom line was I was missing something, perhaps vision, courage or discipline, and maybe a mixture of other things that I was not even aware of.

I allowed the voice to stop me from writing and publishing a book for years. This year, the Lord broke through my identity crisis and tossed out whatever was hindering my breakthrough. He unlocked the faith and grace to accomplish the task of completing this book. I know a lot about the dream killer's voice. Don't listen to it. Listen to the word of God and believe that you can accomplish whatever God puts in your heart to do. This is how I walked into my identity as the author of the book you're reading. I had to rise up.

It may not be easy, but God is omniscient. He knows everything. He has the answer to any question you might ask. He can make sure you get the answer you need.

> "It is the glory of God to conceal a matter; to search out a matter is the glory of kings."
> – Proverbs 25:2 (NIV)

The truth is, God sometimes hides his answers in scriptures and parables. You may have to search the meaning out, but it is there. Others may never see the revelation, but those committed to God and searching for truth will find it.

Get Real

"Be what you is, not what you ain't; 'cause if you ain't what you is, you is what you ain't."
— Luther Price

I love this quote, though I originally heard it a different way and I believe it was attributed to an old Baptist preacher. It said, *"Be who you is, cause if you ain't who you is, then you is who you ain't."*

There is something to be said for being authentic. Think of how much money some people would pay for an authentic Louis Vuitton or Brahmin handbag. However, if you knew it was a counterfeit bag, no matter how real it looked, the value would be substantially diminished.

Now, compare this to yourself. God created you to be your unique self. He doesn't make mistakes. He gave you the look, the hair, the build, the personality, the ability and everything else you needed to accomplish his purpose in your life.

> *"For you created my inmost being; you knit me together in my mother's womb. I praise you because I am fearfully and wonderfully made; your works are wonderful, I know that full well."*
> – Psalm 139:13-14 (NIV)

If God says, you are wonderful, believe it. Don't try to be like someone else. You will never master being someone else. The person you try to be will always beat you at being the best them when you try to put on his or her identity. But you can be number one at being you. If there is an area of your identity that you are concerned about and it is possible to make changes to that area, by all means, do so. As human beings with aspirations, we should be constantly growing and changing for the better.

It is important to know your values, understand your purpose and focus on the way you want to interact with people and the world. We all have an innate desire to make a difference. Discover how you want to do that.

There are various personality tests that are designed to help you discover your strengths and weaknesses, gifts and abilities. Often, they validate what you already believe about yourself. The important thing is not to get bogged down with the processing of all the information you get from these tests. Keep it simple. You know what you like. You know what you love. You know what you desire. A few sessions of self-reflection can confirm that.

Also, don't build around a characteristic that you like, but aren't strong in. Be real. Otherwise, you'll set yourself up for a lifetime of pretending. Remember Polonius' quote from Shakespeare's Hamlet, "This above all: to thine own self be true." Rise up to your true identity.

<u>Re-branding You</u>
Most companies regularly take a look at their bottom-lines or financial reports. Sometimes, they discover that they aren't making the money they have the potential to make, because customers are

not buying their products the way they envisioned. They begin to strategize on what can turn the company around and make it more profitable. One of the things that usually comes up is re-branding. They take a look at what potential customers think about them, what they want customers to think about them, and what to do to make their desires a reality. They then set a project in motion to change any negative perception and promote an exciting positive message.

According to Rolling Stone, Apple, one of the biggest brands we know, started as a computer company, but it was left behind by the personal computer. After years of decline and humbling themselves enough to bring one of the original founders, Steve Jobs, back to the company, Apple began a slow rise back up in the consumer's eye.

In 2001, Apple launched the iPod, and a couple of years later, they launched iTunes. Though initially a struggling computer company, it became "a major player in the entertainment business...changing the way a generation of fans experience portable music."[11]

Nowadays, who hasn't heard of iTunes? Apple has garnered a loyal customer base who seems to think any other phone is simply inferior to the iPhone. That is an example of a highly successful re-branding initiative.

Target, a store that used to compete with Wal-Mart and K-mart, forged ahead in the retail market by, "tapping into Americans' desire for luxury goods by beefing up its selection of trend-forward, stylish products while still offering affordable prices."[12] Today, you may hear Targét instead of Target.

Chapter 8

Rise Up to Covenant

It happened again. There was another royal wedding. Yes, the first one that I remember was Princess Diana and Charles' wedding. It was extravagant and beautiful. Then, there was her son, Prince William and Kate's wedding. Then on May 19, 2018 the world watched as Prince William's brother, Prince Harry and Meghan Markle wed at Windsor Castle, making some declare the California-born actress an American princess. It too is a wedding to be remembered.

I have been to a family member's quaint home wedding with a couple, a minister and a few witnesses. I have been to weddings that appeared to be the social events of the season. The truth is, after all the extravagance, it's all about two people making a covenant agreement.

What is covenant? Covenant is an agreement between two parties. It could refer to a real estate, financial, or marital agreement. Here, we will focus on the marital covenant. Some people use this term rather loosely, but in the past, people understood that a covenant was very serious and was meant to be honored at all costs. A biblical covenant is an agreement between God and his people. This definition implies the importance of covenant. When God's word speaks of promises he makes to his people, you can be assured that he will uphold them.

Leading up to our wedding day, my husband and I attended a group premarital class. That's when our pastor explained to us the concept of covenant marriage. He was honest and told us the possibility of waking up one day after the wedding and wondering why we did it in the first place. He explained that this is when the reality of covenant should kick in and we should remain committed to God and each other, even when we didn't feel like doing so.

Blood Covenant

The term "cutting the covenant" is typically used in regards to people or groups making an agreement.

It is similar to a contract, but it is meant to be binding until death.

Let's look at the steps of a covenant and how it relates to us today.

Step 1 – Exchange coats.
Centuries ago, families would often wear a coat of arms affixed to their coats or other garments. A coat of arms typically represented the unique values and identity of the family and was passed down through the generations. It is a way of establishing pride in one's family, as well as educating young people on what their families stand for. I think we sometimes trust that children will pick up our values through a form of osmosis, just because they live in close contact with us. But instead of leaving it to chance, having a visual of moral conduct, as well as hearing relatives reiterate who their family is and what they stand for, can be a powerful tool. Knowing that you are a part of something bigger than yourself may prompt you to behave in a more socially appropriate way.

When exchanging coats, the two people or their

representatives remove their coats and exchange them. In doing so, they are communicating that they are giving each other their identities; they are giving one another a piece of themselves. They are promising that either of them will be there for the other when they are needed.

> *"No one will be able to stand against you all the days of your life. As I was with Moses, so I will be with you; I will never leave you nor forsake you."*
> — *Joshua 1:5 (NIV)*

When it comes to a relationship with God, you can count on him. It makes me think of the old Jackson 5 song, "I'll Be There." One line says, "Whenever you need me, I'll be there."

> *"All of us have become like one who is unclean, and all our righteous acts are like filthy rags..."*
> — *Isaiah 64:6 (NIV)*

This is us before being redeemed by Christ.

> *"I delight greatly in the LORD; my soul rejoices in my God. For he has clothed me with garments of salvation and arrayed me in a robe of his righteousness..."*
>
> *– Isaiah 61:10 (NIV)*

This is us after Christ. Jesus has exchanged our filthy rags for a robe of righteousness.

Step 2 – Exchange Belts
Have you ever been on a construction site? If so, you have probably seen workers wearing tool belts. These belts are designed to carry the tools that they need while working on certain projects. It would be an inconvenience and an inefficient use of time to have to keep returning to a toolbox.

I don't have a use for a lot of tools outside of the occasional picture hanging task. However, when I've had to go into a hardware store, for me, it was like being in another world. I am amazed at some of the tools they have. Some tools are manually operated and some are power tools, but there seems to be a tool for every imaginable task.

This tool belt is similar to the belts people wore with weapons. When they went to battle, they had everything that they needed. One example is the police duty belt that can carry all their equipment, including radio, taser, handcuffs and handgun. When they are on the street chasing criminals, they need everything within reach in order to apprehend the criminal.

When the covenant partners-to-be exchange belts, they are literally exchanging protection. If one is being attacked the other comes to help fight. This is one reason many people entered blood covenants. If they were weak, they sought alliance with someone stronger.

> *"If you listen carefully to what he says and do all that I say, I will be an enemy to your enemies and will oppose those who oppose you."*
> *– Exodus 23:22 (NIV)*

Now, this is a reason to be in covenant with God. Though he prepares us for spiritual warfare in Ephesians 6, he promises to fight our battles if we listen and obey.

Step 3 – Cut the Covenant
There is always blood shed to seal a covenant. In this ritual, an animal is taken and cut in half the long way. The blood flows down the middle and then the two people walk through the blood, making a figure eight around the halves. After this, they meet back up in the middle to make pronouncements of what should happen to them if they break the covenant. Each party is promising to fulfill the covenant. As I've said, the blood covenant is not meant to be broken.

When Jesus shed his blood, he gave us the opportunity to come into a permanent relationship with him. Although fellowship can be broken us, the relationship we choose to enter in with Jesus is secured by the blood covenant and sealed by the Holy Spirit.

> *"For the life of the body is in its blood. I have given you the blood on the altar to purify you, making you right with the LORD. It is the blood, given in exchange for a life, that makes*

purification possible."
– Leviticus 17:11 (NLT)

The life of Jesus is in his blood. When we say the prayer to accept Jesus, it is really a prayer of giving up ourselves in order to live out God's plan for us. We are, in essence, exchanging our lives for his. By faith, his blood on us gives us spiritual life. We are able to see life with a new, fresh perspective. We are dying to ourselves, while experiencing a spiritual awakening -life.

Step 4 – Mixing the Blood
This step involves each party being cut, usually on the hand or wrist where blood flows freely. They would then clasp their hands together. The blood would mix and they could either suck the blood or have it in a drink mixture. The point was that now the two have become one. There is only one blood for the two people.

Today, we take communion to represent our oneness with Jesus. He said, *"Whoever eats my flesh and drinks my blood remains in me, and I in them." (John 6:56)* We drink wine or juice to represent his blood.

> "For we died and were buried with Christ by baptism. And just as Christ was raised from the dead by the glorious power of the Father, now we also may live new lives."
>
> – Romans 6:4
> (NIV)

As we drink the blood of Jesus, we are putting off our old nature and putting on his nature. The more time we spend with him, the more we take on his being.

Step 5 – Exchange Names
This is evident when couples get married. The wife usually takes the husband's last name, symbolizing that they are now one family. In the past, it was common for people or families who entered into blood covenants to merge their last names.

> "And these signs will accompany those who believe: In my name they will drive out demons; they will speak in new tongues; they will pick up snakes with their hands; and

when they drink deadly poison, it will not hurt them at all; they will place their hands on sick people, and they will get well."
— *Mark 16:17-18 (NIV)*

Have you ever used someone else's name and been granted benefits that you would not have otherwise been afforded? One of the most famous lines children say when talking to their siblings is, "Momma said ..." It's a classic way to get them to move with urgency. The name of Jesus is very influential and powerful in the kingdom of God. If we trust in Jesus, we should be able to use his name to access benefits promised in the Bible.

Step 6 – Make a Scar
After the blood was mingled together, they would often rub ash into the cuts to make it scar as it healed. That scar would be a permanent reminder that the person was in a blood covenant relationship. If anyone wanted to challenge him mentally or physically, they would see the scar and realize the person they were looking at was not the only person they would have to deal with. The scar was likely to make the offender step back and

rethink his/her intentions.

Imagine if you were traveling through a gang infested neighborhood. You might be confronted by members who think you're on their turf and they need to let you know that they run the neighborhood.

> "We know that we are of God, and that the whole world lies in the power of the evil one."
> – I John 5:19 (NIV)

As we maneuver through this world, we must remember that Satan is the ruler of the world. Those who are not submitted to God are under his control. You should not be surprised when people do evil things; however, be reminded that, *"ye are of God, little children, and have overcome them: because greater is he that is in you, than he that is in the world."* – I John 4:4 (KJV)

Like the permanent scar, Satan and his demons recognize the power of God on someone whose life is truly submitted to God. They don't mind taking a shot at us, but when we arise and deal with them from the authority God has given us, they will run. He has been kicked out of heaven before and he doesn't want to have to face the living God.

Step 7 – Giving Terms of Covenant
If you've been to a wedding, you have probably heard the bride and groom either agree to traditional terms of marriage or read their own vows. The traditional vows include, "For better, for worse, for richer, for poorer, in sickness and in health, until death do us part."

Each party's assets and liabilities are brought to the table. Money that belonged to one of them, now becomes the property of both of them. The same goes for debts. They are now both responsible for one another's debt. This is what happens when we accept Christ Jesus into our lives, except he is the responsible party in this covenant relationship. He offered us tremendous benefits, while taking on the debt of our sins.

> *"He forgave us all our sins, having canceled the charge of our legal indebtedness, which stood against us and condemned us; he has*

taken it away, nailing it to the cross."
– Colossians 2:13-14 (NIV)

What a wonderful savior Jesus is! You know how it is when you're in financial debt. There is a similar weight that is carried when you know you have done wrong by God, and you're just waiting for him to punish you. However, what Jesus did was remove the dark cloud from hovering over you. He paid your debt. He took your place. You no longer have to look over your shoulder, wondering how God is going to get you for the displeasing things you've done. They are now covered in the blood of Jesus. Poof! They're gone. You are all clean. You have a fresh start.

Step 8 – Eat a Memorial Meal
At the wedding reception, the bride and groom feed each other cake, and with arms entwined, they drink wine. The memorial meal for blood covenant partners was similar. They broke bread and ate. After that, they drank wine. This tradition represents one giving themselves to the other person, just as communion represents us eating the body of Jesus and drinking his blood. It too is

symbolic of us taking in all of Jesus and giving him ourselves. You've probably heard the saying, "Let's break bread together." It connotes the power of establishing a relationship by sharing a meal.

Step 9 – Plant a Memorial
Trees can be planted to create beautiful landscape patterns, to produce fruit or to produce shade. There is another reason people plant trees and it's to memorialize an event. Occasionally, couples choose to have a tree planting ceremony as a symbol of their union.

Tree plantings also took place for some blood covenant rituals. For both events, the growing tree represented the growing relationship between the couples or covenant partners. The roots would soak in water and nourishment as they sought to go deeper into the earth to stabilize the tree. Through the years, the tree would endure the changes of seasons and the storms of life, and yet, it would continue to stand. What a perfect example of any lasting relationship. You spend time with one another, offering a safe place and nurturing words to help each other grow and overcome the challenges of life. Imagine going through a rocky time in your relationship and you look outside and see the tree that you planted standing tall and flourishing. Perhaps, you will think about your troubles and decide to look for options that, in the end, allow you to continue to stand.

There's no specific order that these steps have to be done in. The important part is that all the parties involved understand that a blood covenant runs deep. It is not a frivolous ceremony. It is a commitment made, not only to your partner, but to God. Usually breaking the covenant is punishable by various curses and death, but God knew that we would not be perfect, so he made a provision for us.

> *"If we confess our sins, he is faithful and just and will forgive us our sins and purify us from all unrighteousness."*
> *– I John 1:9 (NIV)*

Chapter 9

Rise Up and Rest

My love for math blossomed when I was in elementary school. There was something about 2+2=4 and other equations that intrigued me. I think what I liked the most was the satisfaction of reaching *the* answer. There was always an exact answer. I even enjoyed working the problems to discover the value of any variables. Math just makes sense to me. In life, there are a lot of variables that play an important role in whether or not we are successful in our endeavors. As we attempt to work through our problems, there is not always an exact answer. Circumstances fluctuate, and life doesn't stop. It is constantly in motion. Even if you stop and go to sleep tonight, you don't wake up in the morning and continue in time where you left off. No. When you wake up in the morning, it will be tomorrow. Time is unforgiving. It marches forward. We need to be continually learning and growing, making personal improvements so that when opportunity comes, we can make a difference in our world.

Invitation to Rest

Some people do life like a pinball machine. That's the arcade game where you pull a plunger and let it go. It then propels a small steel ball into the field of play on the game. The ball bounces on various bumpers, bells ring and scores rise. Your job is to then use your fingers on either side of the game to control the flippers, so that when the ball starts to roll towards the gutter, you use the flipper to push it back up into the field of play. You do this in hopes of garnering more points.

There are some people who go through life unable to truly enjoy the good times, because they keep waiting for the steel ball to fall on them and ruin all their accomplishments. Then again, there are other people who are always in pursuit of something. They can't enjoy life because they are always trying to score big in business, investments and relationships. They are so busy juggling all of their interests, they have no time for a period of solitude or a time of peaceful refreshing. They are always busy on defense, controlling the levers to keep all the balls in play. They may experience some satisfying wins, but these people can become overwhelmed and stressed, but some of them enjoy the grind.

> "Then, because so many people were coming and going that they did not even have a chance to eat, he said to them, "Come with me by yourselves to a quiet place and get some rest."
>
> – Mark 6:31 (NIV)

In this passage, Jesus is speaking to the disciples after he had been teaching in the synagogue. The disciples had just returned from ministering to people by preaching repentance, delivering the oppressed from demons and healing the sick. Jesus knew that they had been working hard with no chance to eat. He invited them to a quiet place to get some rest.

Even Jesus realized that our human bodies can only do so much before we need to refuel and get some rest. In the scriptures, you can find times when Jesus got alone in a quiet place. Though he was fully

God and fully man on Earth, he chose to suppress the supernatural God side, live from the mortal man side and be an example to us of how to live as Christians in the world. So, if Jesus needed a rest from the activity of the world, so do we.

Internal Activity

> *"For when we came into Macedonia, we had no rest, but we were harassed at every turn — conflicts on the outside, fears within."*
> *– 2 Corinthians 7:5 (NIV)*

Paul too lets us know that even the work of ministry can be challenging. Not only are there all the conflicts that come to us, we also have the challenge of dealing with our own fears. Sometimes, the mental anguish caused by the negative dialogue between our ears is enough to make us question our purpose.

"There is a war going on and your mind is the battlefield." The devil "begins by bombarding our mind with a cleverly devised pattern of little nagging thoughts, suspicions, doubts, fears, wonderings, reasonings and theories." (The Battlefield of the Mind, Joyce Meyer). If we were to take the rabbit trail of any one of those thoughts, they could lead us to places of pain and heartache. That's why we must be proactive and make room for regular quiet time in our lives. This time can be used for worship, prayer, bible reading, listening to God and resting in his presence.

This regular time with God can be the glue that holds you together mentally and physically as you conquer the day ahead. As you develop this habit, you'll find that you can even find a place of rest within yourself, while surrounded by the commotion in your atmosphere.

A Resting Place
When children are having a tough day, they often escape to a happy place. It is a place where they can get their minds off the bad things they've experienced. This place could be in a book or in a treehouse. It's not important where the place is, just that there is a place. Sometimes, it takes more than a happy place to heal a wounded soul. You need some time in the presence of the Lord; you need a

resting place. If you are in a relationship with the Lord, you always have access to a resting place.

> *"The fear of the Lord leads to life; then one rests content, untouched by trouble."*
> *— Proverbs 19:23 (NIV)*

Doesn't the thought of being able to rest mentally and physically sound inviting? How about a place where trouble is blocked from reaching you? According to this verse, it can be a reality if you fear the Lord. This type of fear is not about being afraid. Instead, this fear represents a reverence and a respect for God that makes you want to love, serve and obey him. You recognize that he is God Almighty.

Entering In

We've talked about the resting place, but how do we actually enter into rest in his presence?

> *"This is how we know that we belong to the truth and how we set our hearts at rest in his presence...if our hearts do not condemn us, we have confidence before God and receive*

from him anything we ask, because we keep his commands and do what pleases him."
– 1 John 3:19-22 (NIV)

We can see in this scripture that entering into rest has much to do with our own confidence. Think about when you have done something that is against God's expectations. If you are a believer, you probably felt a tug in your heart, alerting you that what you did was wrong. You may even feel guilt or shame for your action. At unexpected times during the next few days, this guilt may come back to mind, along with negative feelings about yourself and what God must think. You might even begin to ask yourself, "Why would God answer my prayers knowing what I did?" Your Holy Spirit affected conscious is determined to make sure that you feel uncomfortable about what you did. This feeling is likely to help deter you from making the same choice in the future. The truth is you could confess your sin and receive God's forgiveness and then carry on, but your own conscience must be overcome. It's a lot like forgiving yourself. Sometimes, it takes your feelings a while to catch up with the choice to forgive.

> "Therefore, since the promise of entering his rest still stands, let us be careful that none of you be found to have fallen short of it."
> – Hebrews 4:1 (NIV)

This scripture tells us that entering in God's rest is a promise. The opportunity to enter in is for everyone, but the scripture warns that there is a possibility that we can miss out on the experience. What is it that could make us miss out?

> "For we also have had the good news proclaimed to us, just as they did; but the message they heard was of no value to them, because they did not share the faith of those who obeyed."
> – Hebrews 4:2 (NIV)

It is evident that simply reading that God promised us this rest and going through the motions are not beneficial. The missing ingredient is faith in Jesus Christ. The word of God is ultimately ineffective for us unless we are in relationship with his son, Jesus.

If you are not certain that you have a

relationship with Jesus and you want to have one, you can say the following prayer:

God, I confess that I have sinned against you, because I have failed to believe in Jesus. Today, I want to submit myself under the headship of Jesus. Thank you for sending Jesus, my Savior. Thank you for Jesus shedding his blood, dying on the cross and rising up to pay the price for my sins. In Jesus' name, Amen.

If you said this prayer, you are now a child of God with all the benefits. The promise to enter his rest is for you. As you learn more about Jesus, you can expect to hear him in your heart, giving you direction for your life. He will order your steps. Your job is to learn his voice and follow it. He says his sheep hear his voice.

<u>A Voice of Peace</u>
I live in Alabama where tornadoes seem to make an appearance every year. On April 27, 2011, a few wise residents were monitoring the tornado on the ground as it traveled from Tuscaloosa to

Birmingham, leaving a trail of destruction in its wake. According to weather.gov, "there were 29 confirmed tornadoes in Central Alabama on this day, and 62 confirmed tornadoes across the State of Alabama." Now, when the weather report says there is a possibility of severe weather and tornadoes, people in my area have learned to pay attention. It is comforting when we hear that the threat has passed. We depend on the voice of the weather reporter to alert us of impending emergencies.

This is how God wants us to depend on him. He wants us to be tuned in to him, listening to what he has to say. He is committed to guiding us in the way we should go, and he is expecting us to hear and obey him.

> *"For God does speak — now one way, now another — though no one perceives it."*
> *– Job 33:14 (NIV)*

If you are trying to hear an interview on the radio, but you have the dial set to the wrong station, you will miss the interview. Rest allows us to empty our hearts and minds of issues that may be monopolizing our thoughts. This leaves space for us to tune into God's frequency. The information he speaks to us can prevent mishaps, solidify relationships, and change the course of our lives. Whether you hear God during a time of prayer or while you're out for a leisurely walk, it is a wonderful experience to know that the God of the universe takes the time to love and direct you on the best path for your life. Knowing that you are in the will of God can be the best antidote for peace.

Assurance

Have you ever checked your bank account before going shopping or on a vacation? It is reassuring when you know that you have enough funds to pay for the fun you're planning to have without causing yourself financial hardship. Once I was going to use a coupon that I was not certain that applied to an item. It turned out that the item I wanted was listed in the very small print on the back of the coupon as an item not covered in the sale. I was disappointed, but the next time I had a coupon I wanted to use, I made sure to read the small print before going to the store. Then, I could be assured that it could be used for the purchase I intended to make.

Sometimes, people have trouble trusting in a God they cannot see. They want to see and touch a flesh and blood God, but God is a spirit. Those who worship him must worship him in spirit and truth. Without faith, it is impossible to please God. You must believe in Jesus before you experience the benefits he offers you.

> *"I write these things to you who believe in the name of the Son of God so that you may know that you have eternal life."*
> *– I John 5:13 (NIV)*

Outside of the benefits on Earth you qualify for as a child of God, you also receive eternal life. After passing on to the afterlife, you bypass hell and go to heaven to live forever where everything is perfected.

Our God is awesome. He is everywhere. He is all powerful and he knows everything. Isn't that the kind of God we want to serve? Thanks to what Jesus did for us, we now have the opportunity to boldly enter into God's presence. God thought of everything. When Adam and Eve sinned, and every person born after them was affected, God had a plan. He sent Jesus to forever remove sin and its punishment from every person who would believe and receive him.

To anyone who is unsure about giving Jesus a chance, I dare you to try him. Decide to go all in and trust him. Ask him to help you and then, watch how he shows up and displays his love for you. He's for real. If you have already made the commitment to live for Jesus, now it's time for you to go to the next level. God never intended for us to come to him and just live an easy, self-focused life. No, God expects us to grasp hold of his vision and use our abilities to accomplish his will, telling everyone about him and what he offers to believers.

Think of a friend you know very well. If someone told you that she did something that was out of character for her, you might say, "Oh, I know she didn't do that. She's not that kind of person." Your immediate reaction might be to disagree with the person and try to assure him or her that the behavior being addressed does not represent your friend. That's the kind of relationship Jesus wants with you. He wants to be your friend. He wants you to get to know God and his ways so well that if anyone says something untrue about him, you will be willing to stand up and say, "That's not the God I serve. My God doesn't do things like that."

People sometimes say that God made us sick, so we could learn something he's trying to teach us. Many of us grew up with this kind of teaching, but as we grow in our personal relationships with God, we realize that this is not his character. He is a good, good God. That's not to say that he won't use the circumstances in our lives for good, but he doesn't cause bad things to happen to us. Think about it, as a parent would you make your child sick, and possibly have to go to the hospital so he would learn a lesson? God would be worse than most parents to do that to his children.

> *"Let us draw near with a sincere heart in full assurance of faith, having our hearts sprinkled clean from an evil conscience and our bodies washed with pure water."*
> *– Hebrews 10:22 (ESV)*

God desires a relationship with you. He was willing to let Jesus pay your debt for sins past, present, and future, leaving you cleansed and guilt-free. What he did allows you to live in a place of inner peace.

> *"Since we have been justified through faith, we have peace with God through our Lord Jesus Christ."*
> *– Romans 5:1 (NIV)*

Jesus' action gives you the ability to live in a state of restfulness. You don't have to be worried about what's going to happen or not going to happen in your life. You can simply trust God to work on your behalf and lead you in the way you should go. Operating from this place of rest allows you to handle your responsibilities and the challenges of life with grace. Regardless of the circumstances that surround you, you can rise up and rest.

Chapter 10

Rise Up to Success

How do you rise to success? Whether you are beginning or beginning again, the following story, excerpted from *Think and Grow Rich: A Black Choice* by Dennis Kimbro, may enlighten you as you begin your journey to success.

> An old African sage, wise and influential, lived on the side of a mountain near a lake. It was common practice for the people of the village to seek his advice. The old man spent many hours sitting in front of his small hut, where he rocked in a crude rocking chair made of branches and twigs. Hour after hour he sat and rocked as he thought.
>
> One day he noticed a young African warrior walking on the path toward his hut. The young man walked up the hill and stood erect before the sage. "What can I do for you?" the old man said. The warrior replied,

"I was told by those in the village that you are very wise. They said that you can give me the secret to happiness and success."

The old man listened, then gazed at the ground for several moments. He rose to his feet, took the boy by the hand, and led him down the path back toward the lake. Not a word spoken. The young warrior was obviously bewildered, but the sage kept walking. Soon they approached the lake, but did not stop. Out into the water the old man led the boy. The farther they walked, the higher the water advanced. The water rose from the boy's knees to his waist, then to his chin, but the old man said nothing and kept moving deeper and deeper. Finally the lad was completely submerged. At this point the wise man stopped for a moment, turned the boy around, and led him out of the lake and up the path back to the hut. Still not a word was spoken. The old African sat again in his creaky chair and rocked to and fro.

After several thought-provoking minutes, he

looked into the boy's questioning eyes and asked, "Young man when you were in the lake, underwater, what was it that you desired most?"

Openly excited, the boy replied, "Why, you old fool, I wanted to breathe!"

Then the sage spoke this world: "My son, when you want happiness and success in life as badly as you wanted to breathe, then you will have found the secret."

How bad do you want success?

What's Your Story?
What exactly is success? Dictionary.com defines it as "the accomplishment of one's goals." I believe that to be truly successful and fulfilled, you must set the right goals, things that are important to you. You will tend to move toward those things you focus on. Don't just assume that success for you is what the world touts. When you reach that goal line, it should be meaningful to you.

I love the ESPN 30 for 30 stories. Watching sports is entertainment in itself, but when you watch the story of these athletes and coaches, it adds another dimension to the game. These stories often tell what their childhoods were like and the obstacles they had to overcome to reach the success they are experiencing. When you reach a level of success, don't let it be just an empty win for the record books, but make sure there is a meaningful story behind the story ... your story.

<u>A Calling</u>
I didn't really want to do it, but I knew it was coming. For weeks, it had been creeping into our conversations. I could tell God was dealing with my husband. He has a heart for helping people, and he could see that some things could be done better to benefit the people of our city. Then, one day, he told me that he felt like God was leading him to run for mayor. *Oh no,* I thought to myself. I knew that commitment would put some of my plans on hold and cause some major changes in my schedule. However, I am never one to discount what God may be doing, so I agreed to be in prayer about it. We each began to petition the Lord for confirmation

that this was God, or this was not. I asked God to speak as well as have us on one accord. He did. After a short time, I felt like God impressed upon me that he indeed was in this and we had no choice but to follow his leading.

We held a kickoff event to commence the campaign, and we were on our way. We had speaking engagements, debates, fundraisers and more. There was a lot going on, but God was faithful. He supplied me with the grace and stamina to support my husband throughout the campaign. That, to me, was another confirmation that we were in his will. We believed we could win, but in the end, we were not declared the winner. Apparently, God had another plan. Some people would question God, believing if he told us to enter the race, he would have ensured our success in it. I choose to believe that we are winners. Though our goal for the race was to win, our ultimate goal was to obey God. I believe that my husband shared the message he felt God put in his heart and the name of the Lord was lifted up. To me, that was success as I define it, and I am very proud of my husband. When you and I obey God, we win in so many ways.

> *"But if anyone obeys his word, love for God is truly made complete in them. This is how we know we are in him."*
>
> *– I John 2:4-5 (NIV)*

<u>Acknowledge God</u>
Whenever you are making a decision, it is a good idea to inquire of the Lord God. Since he is omniscient, his opinion and direction could prove invaluable in everything, from making a job decision to choosing who you will marry.

In the Old Testament, the Israelite's kings and leaders often inquired of the Lord before they went into battle. An example is when David became king over the Israelites, the Philistine army went looking for him.

> *"Now the Philistines had come and spread out in the Valley of Rephaim; so, David inquired of the Lord, "Shall I go and attack the Philistines? Will you deliver them into my hands?" The Lord answered him, "Go, for I will surely deliver the Philistines into your hands." So, David went to Baal Perazim, and*

there he defeated them. He said, "As waters break out, the Lord has broken out against my enemies before me." So that place was called Baal Perazim. The Philistines abandoned their idols there, and David and his men carried them off. Once more the Philistines came up and spread out in the Valley of Rephaim; so David inquired of the Lord, and he answered, "Do not go straight up, but circle around behind them and attack them in front of the poplar trees. As soon as you hear the sound of marching in the tops of the poplar trees, move quickly, because that will mean the Lord has gone out in front of you to strike the Philistine army." So, David did as the Lord commanded him, and he struck down the Philistines all the way from Gibeon to Gezer.

– 2 Samuel 5:18-25 (NIV)

There are different kinds of battles. These scriptures represent an example of a physical battle, but in life, we come up against enemies in many situations. It's important to know that God doesn't always remove the obstacles, but he works with us to overcome them. When you find yourself facing a challenge, inquire of the Lord. Just ask him what to do and wait for an answer.

As you can see in this example, one of the first things David did when the Philistines came looking for him was to inquire of the Lord. He just asked him in so many words, "Should I attack them? Will I win?" In his own way, God answered, "Sure. You will win." I love the straight forward communication. God loves us and wants to communicate with us, not confuse us. Give him a chance by inviting his input and direction.

There was another time that the Philistines came up against Israel and David again inquired of the Lord as he'd done once before. This time, the Lord gave specific directions of how he should attack them. Instead of going straight up against them, he was advised to circle around and attack them from behind; he was to do this in front of the poplar trees. Notice that in seeking God's advice, one time is not always enough, even in similar situations. God knows the intent of the heart and the plans of your enemies. And he knows the best way to defeat them.

Sometimes, we can be tempted to go our own ways, but in doing so, we are acting as if we know better than God. This is called sin and it dulls our senses, so that it is harder for us to sense God's presence and hear his voice. This should be a scary place to be for a believer who is ultimately dependent on God.

Dominion

"You were created to excel, not fail! That is your divine potential!" said Bishop Jim Lowe. This is God's plan for you. He wants you to experience great success so he can show you off to others and they will know how great your God is. God has continually given us permission to be great.

> *"Then God blessed them, and God said to them, 'Be fruitful and multiply; fill the earth and subdue it; have dominion over the fish of the sea, over the birds of the air, and over every living thing that moves on the earth.'"*
> *– Genesis 1:28 (ESV)*

Even when Adam and Eve were on Earth, God's plan was for them to have dominion over every living thing on Earth, as well as the fish of the sea and birds in the air.

> *"Behold, I give you the authority to trample on serpents and scorpions, and over all the power of the enemy, and nothing shall by any means hurt you."*
> – Luke 10:19 (KJV)

Did you realize that, as a believer, God has given you authority over the power of the enemy? You don't have more power than the enemy, but you have authority that he must submit to. You may have children that have grown bigger and taller than yourself, but they still listen to you, because they recognize your authority as a parent. Likewise, when you act and speak in faith, the devil flees.

My church has a large congregation and after service, there is usually a policeman at the intersection as we exit the parking lot. This officer may not be the biggest, toughest looking man that we have seen, but because of his badge, we recognize that we should follow his directions. His badge represents his authority. Usually, there is a municipality or other government backing the officers. This is much the same as it is when we are dealing with the enemy. In the name of Jesus, we can speak to the things or situations representing the enemy. We have been given authority and those things and situations must obey. Is this the way things work in your life? Are you ruling and having dominion over ungodly influences in your life? I have to ask myself that sometimes. We should be, but it is possible to get caught off guard sometimes.

> *"Be alert and of sober mind. Your enemy the devil prowls around like a roaring lion looking for someone to devour."*
> — *1 Peter 5:8 (NIV)*

The enemy is unable to get the best of everyone, only those who are unaware of the authority they have been given or those who refuse to use it.

> *"Submit yourselves, then, to God. Resist the devil, and he will flee from you."*
> — *James 4:7 (NIV)*

Just know that understanding our authority and using it to counter the hindrances that come against us is a key to success. Use your authority to rise up and succeed.

Promotion Time

If we have been walking with the Lord a long time, it's time that we see some major fruit in our lives.

> *"But the Holy Spirit produces this kind of fruit in our lives: love, joy, peace, patience, kindness, goodness, faithfulness, gentleness, and self-control. There is no law against these things!."*
> – *Galatians 5:22 (NLT)*

In reality, it has less to do with the amount of time you have been a Christian, than the level to which you have chosen to submit to the Lord.

> *"For whoever wants to save their life will lose it, but whoever loses their life for me will find it."*
> – *Matthew 16:25 (NIV)*

When we accepted Jesus, we signed up for him to be the Lord of our lives.

When my children were little, and they did something they shouldn't have done, I would sometimes say, "Now, you are too old to be acting like that. You know better." It appears that God feels a similar way towards us.

> *"We have much to say about this, but it is hard to make it clear to you because you no longer try to understand. In fact, though by this time you ought to be teachers, you need someone to teach you the elementary truths of God's word all over again. You need milk, not solid food! Anyone who lives on milk, being still an infant, is not acquainted with the teaching about righteousness."*
> *– Hebrews 5:11-13 (NIV)*

The writer, believed to be Paul, is attempting to explain something spiritual to others. He then admits that it is hard to make his point clear because they are not trying to understand. I think we have to beware that this can happen in different stages of life. I've certainly experienced a time in my life where I was in a comfortable place. I felt like I had mastered being a Christian. One day, a neighbor of mine who happened to be of a different religious persuasion attempted to sway me to her beliefs. I didn't budge, but after we parted ways, I asked myself, "As a Christian, what makes me different from any neighbor on the street who is not a believer in Christ?"

> *Brothers and sisters, I could not address you as people who live by the Spirit but as people who are still worldly—mere infants in Christ. I gave you milk, not solid food, for you were not yet ready for it. Indeed, you are still not ready. You are still worldly. For since there is jealousy and quarreling among you, are you not worldly?"*
> – *I Corinthians 3:1-3 (NIV)*

God says we are acting like mere infants; the KJV says mere men. We are supposed to be men and women, operating under the power of God supernaturally. We should be using what we have learned to overcome our own issues. Infants are constantly looking for their needs to be met. Mature people are busy trying to help meet the needs of others.

Yes, I admit that I was one of those infants spiritually. However, the question I asked myself started me on a new phase of my journey towards God. I was no longer satisfied with the status quo. I was tired of wearing the mask, smiling while I was hurting. I knew there had to be more to God and Christianity than pretending that everything was going great when it wasn't. It was as if I felt God needed me to pretend to protect his reputation. I was so deceived, but thank God, the new journey solidified my personal relationship with Jesus. I discovered that there are truly so many facets of God that I can continue to learn more of him each day. There is so much more to the Christian life than I could have ever imagined, and I am still learning and growing.

It is so important that we take responsibility for wherever we are in our spiritual walk. It is never too late to grow in the Lord and commit ourselves to learning more about God. His plan was that the work Jesus did while he walked the Earth would continue after he returned to God. As believers, we are the ones who are tasked with the responsibility of carrying out God's plan on Earth. We have to grow up and go out. It's time that we be about the Father's business. This is success.

> *"Keep this Book of the Law always on your lips; meditate on it day and night, so that you may be careful to do everything written in it. Then you will be prosperous and successful.*
> *– Joshua 1:8 (NIV)*

This scripture tells us how to be successful. Remember, the world's way to success may be different, but God's way is based on his word. We need to meditate on it and get it down into our spirits. That's when we begin to speak the word of God from faith. Results are sure to follow. I don't know God's timing, but I know he is faithful.

> *"In everything he did he had great success, because the Lord was with him."*
> *– I Samuel 18:14 (NIV)*

Continue to walk with the Lord. Ready. Set. Go. Let's rise up to success.

Final Message

"and that they will come to their senses and escape from the trap of the devil, who has taken them captive to do his will."
– 2 Timothy 2:26 (NIV)

We have an enemy and he does not want us to complete the good works that God has already prepared for us. One of his tactics is to lull us into complacency.

The ebb and flow of life have a way of drawing us into a concessional lifestyle where we can choose to settle for less than God's best. Rarely are we aware that we are making this choice or if there are consequences for doing so. If we do not remain alert, the acceptance of certain excuses and unfounded beliefs will lead us on a subtle decline into our comfort zones. If this has happened to you, you may be thinking, "There's got to be more to life." May this book be the catalyst to cause you to wake up and rise up. Destiny is calling.

Notes

1. Christine Caine. "Possessing the Promised Land" at Church of the Highlands. 41:06 June 3, 2015. https://www.churchofthehighlands.com/media/message/possessing-the-promised-land
2. Dale Carnegie. Career Coach: The Power of Using a Name. The Washington Post. January 12, 2014. https://www.washingtonpost.com/business/capitalbusiness/career-coach-the-power- of-using-a-name/2014/01/10/8ca03da0-787e-11e3-8963-b4b654bcc9b2_story.html?utm_term=.64efcfcb8e1d
3. https://en.wikipedia.org/wiki/Jehovah-nissi
4. https://en.wikipedia.org/wiki/Jehovah-nissi
5. What do Americans Really Think About the Bible? Barna, April 10, 2013. https://www.barna.com/research/what-do-americans-really-think-about-the-bible/
6. http://www.healthways.com/blog/topic/purpose-well-being
7. https://www.npr.org/sections/health-shots/2014/07/28/334447274/people-who-feel-they-have-a-purpose-in-life-live-longer
8. https://www.ncbi.nlm.nih.gov/pmc/articles/PMC3

389510/

9. https://www.health.harvard.edu/mind- and-mood/how-your-attitudes-affect-your-health

10. https://www.cbsnews.com/news/mothers-forgiveness-gives-convict-second-chance/

11. https://www.rollingstone.com/culture/features/25-incredible-reinventions-in-pop- culture#apple

12. https://www.rollingstone.com/culture/features/25-incredible-reinventions-in-pop-culture#apple.